ALBERT EINSTEIN

POCKET
GIANTS

ALBERT
EINSTEIN

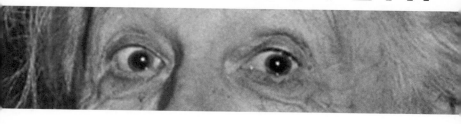

POCKET
GIANTS

ANDREW
MAY

Cover image © ARTHUR SASSE/AFP/Getty Images

First published 2016

The History Press
The Mill, Brimscombe Port
Stroud, Gloucestershire, GL5 2QG
www.thehistorypress.co.uk

British Library Cataloguing in Publication Data.
A catalogue record for this book is available from the British Library.

ISBN 978 0 7509 6380 0

Typesetting and origination by The History Press
Printed and bound in Malta, by Melita Press.

Contents

Introduction

A Giant of Science

'... elementary laws from which the cosmos can be built up by pure deduction.'

Einstein[1]

Few people will be surprised to see Albert Einstein featuring in this series of *pocket GIANTS*: 'You don't have to be Einstein to work that one out.' His name has become a byword for genius, even amongst those who have only the vaguest idea of who he was or what he did. He may have been the greatest scientist of the twentieth century: the point is debatable. What is beyond dispute, however, is that Einstein was the most *famous* scientist of that century – and probably the most instantly recognisable scientist of all time.

What did Einstein do to gain his reputation as a great scientist? How and why did he become such an international celebrity? It might be imagined that the answer to the second question follows automatically from the first, but the truth is not so straightforward. The popular fascination with Einstein becomes harder, not easier, to understand in light of the highly abstract and specialised nature of his scientific work.

First and foremost, Albert Einstein was a thinker. As he himself said: 'What is essential for a man like me is *what* he thinks and *how* he thinks, not what he does or experiences.'[2] In Einstein's case the 'how' was particularly important. He consciously employed a form of reasoning known as deduction, which was common in philosophy but disparaged by most scientists. The idea is to start with an initial proposition and carry it through to its logical conclusion. The strength of the approach lies in the fact that the outcome is necessarily true – not just 'likely' – if the starting premise is true. Its weakness – and the reason other scientists shied away from it – is that a false premise will inevitably lead to a false conclusion. Einstein, however, was confident he could select a valid starting point through pure intuition:

> The intuitive grasp of the essentials of a large complex of facts leads the scientist to the postulation of a hypothetical basic law or laws. From these laws, he derives his conclusions.[3]

> The supreme task of the physicist is to arrive at those universal elementary laws from which the cosmos can be built up by pure deduction. There is no logical path to these laws; only intuition.[4]

Einstein's genius lay in his ability to start in the right place and think his way through to a logical conclusion no matter how counter-intuitive it might appear. The only experiments he conducted were 'thought experiments' – mental images of what and how things *must* happen if certain fundamental postulates were correct. Virtually all the work for which he is remembered used this approach. The result was not just a revolution in science but a series of revolutions. Almost single-handedly, Einstein transformed the way the world now thinks about light, matter, space and time.

One discovery more than any other is associated with Einstein: his theory of relativity. In spite of the name, this is not so much concerned with what is relative as with the invariants of nature – things that are the same everywhere. There are really two distinct theories, special relativity and general relativity, which will be discussed in detail in Chapters 4 and 5.

Both theories started with a simple proposition, which Einstein took as self-evident. In the case of special relativity it was the idea that the laws of physics must be identical in any inertial frame of reference – in other words, any co-ordinate system that is stationary or moving at a constant velocity. This was not a new idea, but Einstein was the first person bold enough, and clear-thinking enough, to follow the argument through to its logical conclusion. It all happened in a flash of insight in the spring of 1905, soon after his 26th birthday: 'I suddenly comprehended it ... Five weeks after my recognition of this, the present theory of special relativity was completed.'[5]

General relativity likewise started with a simple – if somewhat less intuitive – proposition: that a local frame of reference falling freely under gravity behaves exactly as if it were an inertial frame (for a full explanation of what this means, see Chapter 5). This idea, which Einstein later referred to as the luckiest thought of his life, occurred to him in 1907. To work out all of its consequences took not five weeks, as with special relativity, but eight years. At the end of that time, Einstein had created his own theory of gravity, usurping that of Newton which had held sway for more than two centuries.

Einstein's theories of relativity are remarkable achievements, both for the extent to which they redefined our basic notions of space and time, and for the unconventional approach he used in formulating them. According to Otto Frisch, one of the outstanding physicists of the following generation, the basic concept of relativity would probably never have occurred to anyone else at the time:

Nothing but the extraordinary power and concentration of Einstein would have been enough. The clue that led to special relativity was one of the great breakthroughs comparable with the achievements of Galileo and Newton – something that only happens once in a few hundred years.[6]

The same is true of general relativity. As the American physicist Kip Thorne put it: 'Without Einstein, the general relativistic laws of gravity might not have been discovered until several decades later.'[7]

It is easy to understand why Einstein is held in such high regard by scientists. The work he did was of fundamental importance, and he succeeded in solving problems that left his peers baffled. But why should that make him a household name? Why is Einstein the one scientist everyone has heard of? The answer is a complex mixture of factors: partly his personality and physical appearance, partly his activities and pronouncements on non-scientific matters, partly the fact of his being in the right place at the right time.

Einstein's fame has very little to do with the specific details of his scientific work. When he first came to public attention, in the 1920s, an understanding of his theories was not seen as a prerequisite for talking about them. Just the opposite in fact – their very obscurity was part of their appeal. Journalists gleefully reported that no more than a dozen[8] – or sometimes a mere three[9] – people in the world were capable of understanding Einstein's theory of general relativity.

Far from being an obstacle, the sheer incomprehensibility of Einstein's work was entirely in tune with the spirit of the 1920s. Relativity, with its disturbingly counter-intuitive consequences, was seen as part of the emerging avant-garde movement, on a par with atonal music and surrealist art. The abstract painter Piet Mondrian described his underlying principle as 'force is geometry'[10] – which could equally well serve as a succinct summary of general relativity. Marcel Proust, who wrote the famously non-linear novel *In Search of Lost Time*, wrote of Einstein: 'It seems we have analogous ways of deforming time.'[11]

Einstein was, in his own way, just as much a rebel against convention as the artists of the avant-garde. He traced his rebellious streak to a particular phase of his childhood, when he had become disillusioned with the teachings of the Bible:

> Through the reading of popular scientific books I soon reached the conviction that much in the stories of the Bible could not be true. The consequence was a positively fanatic freethinking coupled with the impression that youth is intentionally being deceived by the state through lies: it was a crushing impression. Suspicion against every kind of authority grew out of this experience.[12]

In his personal appearance, too, Einstein was more reminiscent of a Bohemian artist than a professional scientist. His long, unruly hair and crumpled clothes made him stand out from the dapper, smartly dressed crowd of the interwar years. As Einstein's biographer Walter Isaacson put it: 'His baggy, comfortable clothes became a symbol of his lack of pretence … He was able to make his rumpled-genius image as famous as Chaplin did the little tramp.'[13]

By all accounts, Einstein was a striking person to meet face-to-face. A vivid description was provided by the British author C.P. Snow, who encountered Einstein for the first time in 1937:

> At close quarters, Einstein's head was as I had imagined it: magnificent, with a great humanizing touch of the comic. Great furrowed forehead; aureole

of white hair; enormous bulging chocolate eyes ... What did surprise me was his physique. He had come in from sailing and was wearing nothing but a pair of shorts. It was a massive body, very heavily muscled: he was running to fat around the midriff and in the upper arms, rather like a footballer in middle age.[14]

If Einstein's appearance was unlike that of many of his peers, so was his attitude to the subject matter he dealt with: 'When I am judging a theory I ask myself whether, if I were God, I would have arranged the world in such a way.'[15] Einstein's correspondence was often sprinkled with references to God – by which, as he clarified on a number of occasions,[16] he meant a rational but impersonal force of nature rather than a sentient creator:

Subtle is the Lord, but malicious he is not.[17]

I want to know God's thoughts – the rest are mere details.[18]

God does not play dice.[19]

Einstein's fondness for talking about God, coupled with his unorthodox deductive methods, led many of his contemporaries to view relativity as a work of philosophy rather than science. When he received the Nobel Prize for Physics in 1922 it was for his work on quantum theory, not relativity. The latter was seen, according to the chairman of the Nobel Committee, as something that 'pertains essentially to epistemology and has therefore been the subject of lively debate in philosophical circles'.[20]

This was a fundamental misunderstanding. Relativity is not simply a philosophical conjecture. It is a rigorous scientific theory with observable, real-world consequences which are not predicted by rival theories. The satellite navigation technology that we use every day in our cars and mobile phones simply would not work unless it took proper account of both special and general relativity.[21]

Intellectuals often shun the limelight, but not Einstein. He relished all the media attention he could get – not because he wanted everyone to know about his scientific work, but because it enabled him to give voice to his strongly held political views. He was a lifelong pacifist, a campaigner for social justice and a proponent of Jewish independence. His worldwide fame gave him a platform from which to promote these causes to the widest possible audience.

Einstein's fame brought him into contact with some of the greatest figures of the twentieth century. He talked politics with Sigmund Freud, Bertrand Russell and Albert Schweitzer. He corresponded with the Queen of Belgium, beginning his letters 'Dear Queen' rather than 'Your Majesty'.[22] He met Franz Kafka, Winston Churchill, Charlie Chaplin – and possibly even Marilyn Monroe, who kept a signed photograph of Einstein with her until her death.

For many people Einstein is the ultimate stereotype of a 'mad scientist', and in some ways this picture is correct.

There are numerous anecdotes showing him to have been absent-minded and otherworldly throughout his life. On one occasion he is said to have phoned his wife with the succinct query, 'Where am I and where am I meant to be?'[23] On another occasion, perhaps less believably, a college secretary is supposed to have received a phone call asking for Einstein's address. When she explained that she wasn't allowed to give it out, the reply came: 'Please don't tell anybody, but I *am* Dr Einstein. I'm on my way home and I've forgotten where my house is.'[24]

Einstein's office in Berlin was a picture of organised chaos:

> His desk was piled high with books and papers, the overloaded shelves dusty with neglect, and the floor visible only in places where gaps remained between piles of books and papers. Yet he always knew exactly where a particular paper or book was kept.[25]

When he moved to America, he was asked what office equipment he would need. Einstein's answer was: 'A desk or table, a chair, paper and pencils ... and a large wastebasket, so I can throw away all my mistakes.'[26] In time the office acquired pictures of the people he most admired: three physicists – Isaac Newton, Michael Faraday and James Clerk Maxwell – as well as Mahatma Gandhi, the Indian civil rights campaigner.

While his public persona conformed to a neat stereotype, Einstein's private life was more complicated.

Many of its details only became public with the release of his private correspondence during the 1980s and 1990s. Prior to this it was known, for example, that he had an extended romance with fellow student Mileva Marić before marrying her in 1903. It was not known, however, that the romance had produced an illegitimate child – a daughter who must have died in infancy or been sent for adoption under a different name, leaving just a few tantalising imprints on the historical record.

Similarly, biographers had always known that Mileva left Einstein in 1914, returning to their previous home in Switzerland while Einstein remained in Berlin. What became clear after the full correspondence came to light is that, shortly before Mileva's departure, her husband had presented her with a long list of conditions beginning, 'You will make sure that my clothes and laundry are kept in good order' and ending 'You will undertake not to belittle me in front of our children'.[27]

As one of Einstein's biographers, Walter Isaacson, puts it, 'Einstein was human, and thus both good and flawed, and the greatest of his failings came in the realm of the personal'.[28] As a young man in his 20s, a colleague had noted that he 'had no understanding of how to relate to people'.[29] Later, a friend described Einstein's interpersonal relationships in the following way:

He had a shy attitude toward everybody. He was gentle, considerate of others, and the opposite of pompous. But I never heard even a close friend call him by his first name. When someone did treat him with undue familiarity, he would shrink back.[30]

A retrospective attempt to psychoanalyse Einstein was made by the British psychologist Anthony Storr in 1976. He concluded that Einstein demonstrated clear schizophrenic tendencies, manifested by his rebelliousness and disregard for authority, his absent-mindedness and coolness towards others, and his lack of interest in creature comforts.[31]

Storr went on to suggest that only a schizophrenic could achieve the level of detachment needed to come up with the theory of relativity. Einstein certainly turned all the established ideas about space and time on their head, forcing his fellow scientists to look at the world from an entirely new perspective. Whether that is the work of a madman or a genius – or both – is for the reader to judge.

1

The Making of a Genius

'A lazy dog who never bothered about mathematics ...'

Hermann Minkowski on Einstein[32]

Albert Einstein was a big-headed child, physically as well as figuratively. When he was born, on 14 March 1879 in the German town of Ulm, his mother initially feared that her baby was deformed because his skull was so large. Einstein's head remained large in proportion to his body even into adulthood. For this reason, photographs often give the impression that he was a short, stocky individual; in fact, at 175cm (or 5ft 9in), he was of average height. It was just his head that was out of the ordinary – both on the outside and the inside.

Einstein was a deep thinker from the start. One of the many myths about him is that he was a slow learner, or perhaps even a backward child. The opposite is true. Certainly, he was late to start talking – but only because he realised there was no point in babbling words at random; he could see that they had to be structured into sentences before they conveyed any useful meaning. As he said later, 'I formed the ambition to speak in whole sentences. I would try each sentence out on myself by saying it softly. Then when it seemed right, I would say it out loud.'[33]

The young Einstein had a short temper. When his sister Maja was born in 1881, she quickly became both his closest companion and the chief target for his tantrums: 'A sound skull is needed to be the sister of a thinker,[34] she remarked later. By the time Maja was born the family had moved to Munich, where Einstein's father and uncle had set up an electrical engineering company. To start with the company did very well. After a few years the Einsteins were able to move into a big new house in an affluent suburb where the two children had a large, sprawling garden in which to play. In 1885, now with 200 employees, the Einstein company provided the first ever electrical lighting system for Munich's famous *Oktoberfest* beer festival.

With the exception of Maja, Einstein tended to remain aloof from other children, looking down on their frivolous antics with disdain. He was particularly contemptuous of boys who played at being soldiers – an attitude that would gradually evolve into a profound dislike of anything military.

At the age of 5 Einstein started at the local Catholic elementary school. This may seem surprising, because his parents were Jewish. They were not, however, strong followers of the Jewish faith, and they were keen to integrate into mainstream German society. The original intention had been to name their son Abraham, after his paternal grandfather, but they decided this sounded 'too Jewish'[35] and settled on Albert instead.

Following the common practice of the day, the school taught children by rote – expecting them to memorise and repeat carefully selected facts. This infuriated Einstein, who was desperate to learn about the things that interested him but wanted to do so in his own way. There were frequent clashes with teachers. On at least one occasion a schoolmaster was forced to duck when a chair was hurled at him by an indignant young Einstein.

The teachers, for their part, were as unimpressed with him as he was with them. He was regarded as inattentive, argumentative and unlikely ever to amount to much. Again, this has contributed to the myth that Einstein was in some sense a weak learner at school. The truth is that Einstein hated being taught; he preferred to work things out for himself.

This attitude continued – possibly even intensified – after Einstein started high school at the age of 10. The curriculum was centred on classical humanities, and the laborious study of ancient Greek and Latin – subjects that did little to stir young Einstein's enthusiasm. He was rescued from utter boredom a couple of years later by a family friend named Max Talmud, who was a decade older than him. Max was an aspiring medical student who, alone among everyone in Einstein's circle at the time, could see potential in this moody, large-headed 12 year old. Week after week he brought Einstein reading material, which the youngster devoured voraciously. There were books on geometry, a subject Einstein loved because of its simple perfection. There were popular accounts of the latest developments in physics, which went far beyond anything Einstein was being taught by his schoolteachers. There was even philosophy. By the time he was 13, Einstein had read and assimilated one of the most challenging philosophical texts of all time: Kant's *Critique of Pure Reason*.

Einstein had finally been set on the right path. Just over a decade later those three subjects – geometry, physics and philosophy – would become the triple pillars underpinning his theory of relativity. Max Talmud had shown him his true destiny. If the matter had been left to his conventionally materialistic parents, he might have ended up as a middle-class businessman like his father.

Germany already had a well-established electrical industry, and the Einstein brothers found themselves in constant competition with giant corporations like AEG and Siemens, so in 1894 they decided to move their entire operation to Milan in Italy, where they felt the market would offer better opportunities. The family duly moved, along with the business – all except for 15-year-old Einstein, who was left behind to complete his schooling in Munich.

Separated from his family by hundreds of miles, Einstein plunged into a bitter depression. He hated school, he hated German politics and he hated the fact that, once he reached the age of 17, he would be forced to enter military service.

So Einstein ran away – but only after he had thought things through and established a clear plan of action. He started by getting a doctor – who just happened to be the older brother of his friend Max – to write a note excusing him from school on the grounds that he was on the verge of a nervous breakdown. The school staff were overjoyed to hear this; they had been looking for a way to get rid of this disruptive student for some time.

On 29 December 1894 the 15-year-old Einstein boarded a train at Munich's Hauptbahnhof and travelled to Italy to rejoin his parents. He told them he planned to renounce his German citizenship and take refuge in Switzerland, where he would train to become a physics teacher. His father was horrified, not because Einstein wanted to move to Switzerland, but because his son was clearly obsessed with physics – 'philosophical nonsense', as he called it.[36] Einstein Senior was a practical man, and he wanted his son to be practical too. Go to Switzerland by all means, but for heaven's sake study a worthwhile subject like engineering!

Einstein ignored his father's advice. He knew exactly what he wanted to do. The place on which he had set his heart was the Swiss Federal Polytechnic Institute in Zurich. This was not, strictly speaking, a university, because it could not award doctoral degrees. Its primary aim was to train students to become teachers. As a federal establishment, however, it was at least as prestigious as Zurich University, and it had a particularly strong reputation in the sciences. When he took the entrance examination in September 1896, Einstein passed it with flying colours; his average grade was higher than that of any other candidate that year. The following month he was ready to start his studies. At 17, he was at least a year younger than most of the other undergraduates.

One might imagine, given that Einstein was finally at an institution of his own choosing, that he would be happy with the quality of the teaching he received. But this was not the case. He was just as critical of the staff of the polytechnic as he had been of his schoolteachers in Munich.

The problem for Einstein was that he had already read more than his teachers about physics. He knew all about the latest ideas and developments, and he wanted a chance to discuss them in class. He was well aware, for example, that thirty years earlier the work of James Clerk Maxwell had put the subject of electromagnetism on the same rigorous mathematical footing that Newton had applied to classical physics in the seventeenth century. Yet Maxwell's equations were never mentioned in Einstein's physics lectures.

The head of physics at the polytechnic was 50-year-old Heinrich Weber, who taught the same curriculum he had learned as a young man. For Einstein and his fellow students, Weber's lectures were more like lessons in history than science. 'We waited in vain for a presentation of Maxwell's theory; Einstein above all was disappointed,' one of them said later.[37]

Weber's correct title, as far as his students were concerned, was 'Herr Professor', but Einstein habitually addressed him as plain 'Herr Weber'. This calculated insult did nothing to endear him to the man who would one day need to be called on for employment references.

The situation with mathematics was not dissimilar. Einstein liked his mathematics professor, a man named Hermann Minkowski, but felt the topics he taught were almost completely irrelevant. He had loved the mathematics he learnt at school – simple algebra and Euclidean geometry – because the concepts seemed so pure and logical to him; as a budding physicist, he could see how those concepts could be applied to the real world. But the more advanced mathematics that were taught by Minkowski, things like tensor calculus and higher dimensional spaces, seemed completely pointless. Minkowski later described Einstein as 'a lazy dog who never bothered about mathematics at all'.[38]

They were both wrong. Hermann Minkowski is remembered today for a discovery that could have been Einstein's, if only he had paid attention in lectures. When Einstein first developed the theory of special relativity in 1905, he did so using rather convoluted algebra. Minkowski noticed that Einstein's equations could take a much simpler form if they were expressed in terms of four-dimensional non-Euclidean geometry: 'Minkowski spacetime' as it is now called. Without that insight – and without other mathematical techniques he had dismissed as irrelevant, such as tensor calculus – Einstein would never have gone on to crack the problem of general relativity.

From earliest childhood and throughout his education, Einstein held strong opinions about what was worth learning and what was not. In most cases his judgement seems to have been accurate, at least as far as his chosen career was concerned. But his neglect of higher mathematics was a regrettable exception, as he admitted later in life: 'It was not clear to me as a student that a more profound knowledge of the basic principles of physics was tied up with the most intricate mathematical methods.'[39]

There were ten other physics students in Einstein's year, and one of them was female. Her name was Mileva Marić.

She was from Serbia, which at the time was part of the Austro-Hungarian Empire. Mileva was three years older than Einstein, but they were quickly attracted to each other. She was as passionate about physics as he was and had fought just as hard to get into the polytechnic – one of the few places of higher education that accepted students of both sexes. She was intelligent, rebellious and moody, just like him. Physically, though, she was less impressive. A pen-picture written by another student described her in the following terms: 'very smart and serious, small, delicate, brunette, ugly.'[40]

Einstein and Mileva became close. They skipped classes – both feeling they could learn more effectively on their own – and spent as much time as they could together. Before long they were talking about marriage. The correspondence between the two became increasingly urgent. In one letter Einstein wrote, 'We understand each other's dark souls as well, and also drinking coffee and eating sausages etcetera.' That Einstein had something specific in mind when he used the word 'etcetera' is suggested by his sign-off to another letter: 'Best wishes etcetera, especially the latter.'[41]

Einstein's parents were horrified, his mother in particular. She had developed a deep dislike of Mileva before she had even met her. The reasons for this are unclear, although there is no shortage of speculation. It may have been the prejudice of a German against a non-German, or of a Jew against a non-Jew (Mileva's family belonged to the Eastern Orthodox branch of Christianity). On the other hand, it may simply have been a case of 'a mother knows best' when it comes to her son's love life. Einstein later described how she 'threw herself on the bed, buried her head in the pillow, and wept like a child' when he first told her of his desire to marry Mileva.[42]

After four years at the polytechnic, Einstein and Mileva took their final examinations in July 1900. Mileva fell short of a pass, due mainly to a poor performance in mathematics. Strictly speaking Einstein fell short too, but he came close enough to scrape through. As a graduate of the polytechnic, he was now qualified to teach and to study for a doctor's degree at Zurich University. Mileva, on the other hand, had to wait another year before she could retake her examinations.

There was still one obstacle for Einstein to overcome before he could apply for a proper job. Although he had lived in Switzerland since 1895, he was not yet a Swiss citizen. The situation was eventually rectified in February 1901 when, just short of his 22nd birthday, Einstein finally passed the gruelling Swiss citizenship test.

By this time all the other students who had graduated in physics along with him had secured good jobs – some as teaching assistants at the polytechnic itself. But for some reason Einstein was unable to follow in their footsteps. He sent off application after application, and they were all rejected. It turned out that 'Herr Weber' was happily telling anyone who asked him that Albert Einstein was unfit for employment.

Einstein was forced to take short-term tutoring assignments in order to earn a living. At the same time, he started work on a PhD dissertation at the University of Zurich. Unfortunately the senior staff there were as wedded to nineteenth-century physics as their counterparts at the polytechnic. For a young man whose head was bubbling over with novel and revolutionary ideas, Einstein faced a long, hard struggle.

In May 1901, Einstein and Mileva went on holiday to Lake Como in northern Italy, not far from the Swiss border. Soon after they returned home, Mileva discovered she was pregnant. The obvious solution would have been for Einstein and Mileva to get married then and there – but for various reasons that was not possible. Einstein's family were still opposed to the marriage; he lacked a permanent job and had little prospect of obtaining one in the foreseeable future; and, in July 1901, when Mileva retook her examination at the polytechnic, she failed for the second year running.

With an immediate marriage out of the question, Mileva decided to go back to her parents' home in Serbia and have the baby there, with as little fuss as possible. Einstein remained in Switzerland to continue his doctoral research and his dogged quest to find proper employment. His letters to Mileva (or 'Dollie', as he liked to call her) were filled with excited talk about their future together: 'Soon you'll be my happy little wife, just watch … Soon I'll be able to take my Dollie into my arms and call her my own in front of the whole world.'[43]

2

A Patent Clerk with Big Ideas

'The discovery of a universal formal principle ...'

Einstein[44]

Einstein moved to Bern in Switzerland in January 1902, drawn by the prospect of a job in the Swiss Patent Office. A few days after his arrival he received a letter from Mileva's family in the Serbian city of Novi Sad, telling him she had given birth to a daughter named Lieserl. He wrote back excitedly: 'Is she healthy and does she cry properly? What are her eyes like? Which one of us does she more resemble?'[45] But the idea of taking the train to Novi Sad, and seeing Lieserl with his own eyes, never seems to have crossed his mind.

Around the same time Einstein heard that Zurich University had rejected the doctoral thesis he had submitted a few months earlier. The text of that thesis has now been lost, and it is tempting to imagine that it represented some momentous scientific breakthrough which the Zurich professors were too hidebound to appreciate, but the truth is probably more mundane. Einstein's earliest published papers, dating from 1901 and 1902, are strong on speculation and weak on content. It seems likely that the rejected thesis would have been similar.

Disappointed but not defeated, Einstein finally started his patent office work as 'Technical Expert Third Class' on

23 June 1902, at a salary of 3,500 Swiss francs per annum (equivalent in spending power to just over £10,000 today). He was expected to sit at his desk for eight hours a day, six days a week, although he was only actually occupied when there were patent applications for him to look over. The rest of the time he was at liberty to get on with his scientific work – an arrangement which suited him perfectly.

A further step forward came in October 1902, when Einstein received an urgent call to visit his gravely ill father in Milan. The latter, on his deathbed, finally gave his blessing for Einstein to marry Mileva. Einstein's mother was unhappy about this, but as it was her husband's dying wish there was little she could do about it.

The wedding took place in Bern on 6 January 1903. The only guests were Einstein's work colleagues. There can be no doubt, however, that the bride's family approved of the union: they are said to have offered a dowry of 100,000 Swiss francs – approximately £300,000 in today's money, or almost thirty times Einstein's annual salary.

The post-wedding celebrations went on well into the night. When the happy couple finally returned to their apartment in the early hours, Einstein – as absent-minded as ever – discovered he had lost his keys. They were forced to ring the bell and wake the landlord.

Although they were now married and living together in Bern, their young daughter was not with them; Lieserl remained with her maternal grandparents in Novi Sad. In August 1903 the worrying news came that she had contracted scarlet fever. Mileva immediately got a train to Serbia. Einstein, whose enthusiasm for parenthood remained abstract, stayed where he was.

Lieserl is mentioned a few times in the ensuing correspondence between Einstein and Mileva, then never again. For decades the child's very existence was forgotten, until Einstein's private papers were published in the 1980s. Although considerable detective work has been put into trying to reconstruct what happened to her, no definitive answer has emerged. One possibility is that Lieserl died from her illness, although no death certificate has been found. Another is that she was discreetly handed over to a friend or family member to be raised under a different name.

The latter outcome seems to be hinted at in a letter Einstein wrote to Mileva in September 1903:

> I am very sorry about what happened with Lieserl. Scarlet fever often leaves some lasting trace behind. If only everything passes well. How is Lieserl registered? We must take great care, lest difficulties arise for the child in the future.[46]

This clearly suggests that Lieserl was still alive, but the words sound like a man talking about a child who was now someone else's problem, not his own. The Lieserl mystery may never be solved.

By the time Lieserl vanished from the scene, Mileva was already pregnant with a second child. Hans Albert Einstein was born in May 1904. He was the first of two sons. His younger brother, Eduard, was born six years later.

Einstein published his first scientific paper in 1901, in a prestigious journal called *Annalen der Physik* (Annals of Physics), which had been in existence since 1799. There was nothing particularly outstanding about Einstein's first foray into scientific research or the sequel he wrote the following year. According to his biographers Michael White and John Gribbin: 'The whole basis of these papers is just plain wrong.'[47]

Nevertheless, Einstein persisted. He produced a steady stream of scientific papers, written at the patent office: another one later in 1902, one in 1903 and one in 1904. They addressed a variety of problems in what at the time was cutting-edge physics. These early contributions were ambitious, audacious – and ultimately forgettable. In some cases, Einstein was simply repeating what, unknown to him, had already been discovered by other scientists. In other cases he was, again, 'just plain wrong'.

The breakthrough came in 1905. In March that year, Einstein submitted a paper to *Annalen der Physik* with the somewhat clumsy title 'On a Heuristic Viewpoint Concerning the Production and Transformation of Light'. The paper was accepted, and it duly appeared in the June issue of the journal. It ushered in the first of the two scientific revolutions for which Einstein would be responsible that year.

The problem he tackled was related to an experimental phenomenon called the photoelectric effect. It was known that under certain circumstances a flow of electrons could be created by shining light on to a metal surface. Three years earlier, in 1902, a Hungarian–German physicist named Philip Lenard had discovered that the energy of the electrons depended not on the brightness of the light – as might be expected – but on its colour. As yet, however, there was no theoretical explanation for this.

Einstein found a way to account for Lenard's observations. He turned to an obscure theory proposed by the German scientist Max Planck in 1900, and almost completely ignored since then. It was called quantum theory – the idea that light energy is contained in discrete packets called 'quanta'. As Einstein put it:

> When a light ray is propagated from a point, the energy is not continuously distributed over an increasing space, but consists of a finite number of energy quanta which are localised at points in space and which can be produced and absorbed only as complete units.[48]

This may not appear particularly revolutionary at first glance. Many people will have encountered the idea that light is made up of particles called photons, and 'photon' is simply the modern name for a quantum of light. But this view seemed at odds with centuries of experimental evidence which demonstrated beyond doubt that light travels through space in the form of a wave. A particle is one thing; a wave is another. Surely light must be *either* a wave *or* a particle – common sense tells us it cannot be both.

The essence of Einstein's genius is that he steadfastly refused to be misled by common sense. He followed logical arguments through to their inevitable conclusions – and if those conclusions deviated from common sense, then it was common sense that needed to be questioned. Light is *both* a wave and a stream of particles – that is the upshot of quantum theory. Although it had been Planck who had first proposed the theory, he had never really believed in it; for him it was simply a convenient mathematical device. But Einstein's work on the photoelectric effect proved quantum theory was real. In due course, it was for this breakthrough – not relativity – that he would win the Nobel Prize in 1922.

At the end of April 1905, Einstein had a second attempt at submitting a doctoral thesis to the Zurich authorities. This time he decided to steer clear of revolutionary topics like quantum theory and relativity. The title of his dissertation was 'A New Determination of Molecular Dimensions', and its subject matter proved conservative enough to meet with approval. His thesis was accepted at the end of July, although his doctorate was not formally awarded until the following January.

The subject of molecules also featured in another of the clumsily titled papers Einstein sent to *Annalen der Physik* in 1905: 'On the Movement of Small Particles Suspended in Stationary Liquids Required by the Molecular Kinetic Theory of Heat'. The paper provided a new analysis of a well-known phenomenon called Brownian motion: the apparently random movement of dust particles suspended in a fluid when viewed through a microscope. Einstein showed this to be due to collisions with the invisibly small molecules making up the fluid. His paper was submitted in May and published just two months later.

By the middle of 1905 Einstein's momentum was established. He had already completed a doctoral thesis and written two major scientific papers that year, with a third on the way. He had discovered the key to success, and it was not the tried and tested scientific method used by all his peers. Einstein had come to favour the deductive approach:

> I despaired of the possibility of discovering the true laws by means of constructive efforts based on experimentally known facts. The longer and the more despairingly I tried, the more I came to the conviction that only the discovery of a universal formal principle could lead us to assured results.[49]

Einstein's uniqueness, and his greatness, lay in the way he thought about the world: the questions he asked himself, the pictures he formed in his mind and the mental steps he took. But that is not to say he worked in complete isolation from the people around him. He was happy to bounce ideas off anyone who could follow his train of thought – friends, colleagues, students ... and above all, his wife.

The extent to which Mileva contributed to Einstein's early work is a controversial subject. Some commentators maintain she had hardly any involvement at all, while others portray her as virtually an equal partner. In their student days they certainly had a vision of their future career together as scientific co-workers: 'When you're my dear little wife we'll diligently work on science together',[50] Einstein wrote to her on one occasion.

Romantic though that notion is, it is much more likely that the ideas attributed to Einstein originated in his own head. But it is certain that Mileva would have acted as a sounding board for these ideas and may have helped to work out many of the fine details. The relationship was probably expressed most clearly by their son Hans Albert (who grew up much closer to his mother than his father): 'Mileva helped him solve certain mathematical problems, but no-one could assist with the creative work, the flow of ideas.'[51]

On another occasion, when asked about his mother's attitude towards Einstein's work, Hans Albert said:

She was very proud of him, but that is as far as it went. It was very hard to understand, because she originally had studied with him and had been a scientist herself. But, somehow or other, with the marriage she gave up practically all of her ambitions in that direction.[52]

Nevertheless, during the early years of their marriage both Mileva and Einstein constantly used the words 'we' and 'our' when referring to his scientific work. In August 1905,

Mileva proudly told her father: 'Not long ago we finished a very significant work that will make my husband world famous.'[53]

The work she was referring to was not Einstein's paper about the photoelectric effect or the one about Brownian motion. It was the third piece Einstein had written that year, which he sent off to *Annalen der Physik* at the end of June and which was duly published in September. 'On the Electrodynamics of Moving Bodies' heralded the second Einsteinian revolution of 1905: the theory of relativity.

3

The Relativity Revolution

'Space by itself, and time by itself, have vanished into the merest shadows ...'

Hermann Minkowski[54]

The principle of relativity is inextricably linked with Einstein's name, not because he invented it but because he rescued it from the brink of oblivion. The basic idea is that there is no such thing as an absolute standard of rest; if two observers are moving relative to each other, they are equally entitled to say 'I am stationary and you are in motion'. Throughout the seventeenth, eighteenth and the first half of the nineteenth century, scientists took this principle for granted – it lay at the heart of the classical physics of Galileo and Newton. But developments in electromagnetism during the latter half of the nineteenth century seemed to imply that relativity was wrong, and that the universe does indeed have an absolute standard of rest. The resulting crisis in physics would eventually culminate in Einstein's greatest triumph.

The basic principle of relativity was first articulated by Galileo (1564–1642) in his *Dialogue Concerning the Two Chief World Systems*, published in 1632. It would be difficult to improve on his original explanation of the principle, which takes the form of a 'thought experiment' worthy of Einstein himself:

Shut yourself in with a friend in the largest room you can find undercover on some large ship … If you throw something to your companion, you will not need to throw it with more force in one direction than another, provided the distances are the same. Jump with both feet across the floor, and you will jump the same distance in any direction. Observe all these effects carefully, even though as long as the ship is stationary there is no reason to expect them to be otherwise than they are. Then have the ship move, at whatever speed you choose; and provided its motion is uniform and not rocking to and fro, you will not notice the slightest change in any of these effects, and none of them would give you any indication of whether the ship was moving or at rest.[55]

In other words, there is no experiment an observer can perform that will determine whether their frame of reference is stationary or moving at a constant velocity. In the jargon of relativity such frames are referred to as 'inertial frames', to distinguish them from non-inertial frames moving with non-constant velocity.

Galileo's principle of relativity is so-called because it means that motion can only ever be measured in a relative sense. An observer can declare their own favoured inertial frame to be 'stationary', but ultimately this is an arbitrary choice – one inertial frame is as good as another. There is no such thing as an absolute standard of rest.

This was important to Galileo because he was trying to dispel the mediaeval myth that the earth was stationary at the centre of the universe. He knew the earth was moving around the sun, and he suspected that the sun itself might be in motion too, but ultimately it was a moot point because all motion is relative.

Galileo's view of the world was put on a rigorous mathematical footing by Isaac Newton (1642–1727) in his seminal work *Philosophiae Naturalis Principia Mathematica* (Mathematical Principles of Natural Philosophy), which was published in 1687. Any lingering doubts that an absolute frame of rest might exist were dispelled, and for almost two centuries no one looked back.

Newton was born the year Galileo died, and Einstein was born the year that another great scientist died – the Scottish physicist James Clerk Maxwell (1831–79). Einstein's work would build on foundations laid by Maxwell, just as Newton's work was based on Galilean underpinnings.

Maxwell's greatest achievement, first published in 1865, was the set of four equations that bear his name. Maxwell's equations pulled together everything that was known about electricity, magnetism and the intimate relationship between them. More than that, Maxwell showed that one solution of his equations took the form of a wave, made up of alternating electric and magnetic fields, which propagated through space with a speed determined by certain fundamental constants of nature. This speed coincided exactly with the measured speed of light, implying that light was a form of electromagnetic wave.

There was a serious problem, though. The equations suggested that the wave travelled at a constant speed, but they did not disclose what this speed was relative to. Yet the principle of relativity, established by Galileo more than two centuries earlier, meant that motion had to be measured *relative to something*.

Physics was faced with one of the biggest theoretical crises in its history. On the face of it, either Galileo was right and Maxwell was wrong, or Maxwell was right and Galileo was wrong. But Galileo's world view had underpinned classical physics since the seventeenth century, and Maxwell's equations enshrined everything that had ever been determined experimentally about electricity and magnetism. It seemed an impossible choice.

Odd as it may seem, a consensus soon emerged that the new theory was correct and the flaw must lie in Galileo's principle of relativity. There was a return to the medieval view of an absolute standard of rest, but now the standard was not the stationary earth at the centre of the universe, but the invisible medium relative to which electromagnetic waves travelled at the speed of light.

The mysterious medium was given a name – 'the ether'. For decades it defied all experimental efforts to detect it. Most physicists, nevertheless, remained convinced that it did indeed exist. They developed increasingly convoluted theories to explain why it could not be detected experimentally.

This was the background against which Einstein wrote his third paper of 1905, 'On the Electrodynamics of Moving Bodies'. He started by asking a question so simple that it had never even occurred to anyone else: what if both Galileo *and* Maxwell are right?

Maxwell's equations say that light travels at a constant speed, usually denoted by the letter c. They do not say what this speed is measured relative to. Galileo's principle of relativity states that an observer carrying out experiments in an inertial frame of reference will always obtain the same results, whatever speed the inertial frame is travelling at.

So what happens if Galileo's observer tries to test Maxwell's equations? If both Maxwell's equations and Galileo's principle are correct, the observer should always get the same result, regardless of their own motion. They should always measure exactly the same value for c, the speed of light.

To Einstein, who had no reason to doubt either Galileo or Maxwell, this proposition seemed self-evident. He used it as the starting point for a chain of deduction which he pursued with relentless logic. By the time he had finished, he found himself in a very strange world indeed. Common sense had fallen by the wayside, just as it had done a few months earlier with quantum theory.

Einstein's version of relativity is just like Galileo's, at the sort of velocities encountered in the everyday world.

It is only when objects move at speeds approaching that of light that the strangeness starts to set in. A spaceship moving at such a speed becomes measurably shorter in length, while time slows down for the people on board. As the speed increases, the mass of the spaceship steadily becomes larger, making it harder and harder to accelerate to higher speeds.

Some of these strange effects had been predicted by other scientists before Einstein, in the context of theories of the ether. But Einstein showed that the ether was unnecessary – the only really fundamental component was c, the speed of light.

It turned out that c is a kind of absolute speed limit for the universe. A material object can approach that speed but never quite reach it. If it did reach it, Einstein's equations say the object would have infinite mass and zero length – an obvious impossibility. An even stranger consequence of Einstein's theory is the 'time dilation' experienced by a fast moving spacecraft. The closer it approaches that critical speed c, the slower time passes for its occupants. To an earthbound observer a spaceship travelling at 99 per cent of the speed of light would take just over four years to reach Alpha Centauri, the nearest star. For the crew members on board, however, the trip would only take six months.

In Galileo's version of relativity, it is motion – the velocity of an object – that is relative. In Einstein's version, time is also relative. Even the seemingly fundamental concept of simultaneity has to be abandoned:

Two events which, viewed from a system of coordinates, are simultaneous, can no longer be looked upon as simultaneous events when envisaged from a system which is in motion relative to that system.[56]

There was a far-reaching truth implicit in Einstein's paper which even he failed to appreciate at first. Ironically for the young revolutionary, it was one of his former professors from Zurich – the mathematician Hermann Minkowski – who was first to grasp what the 'lazy dog' (as he had called his erstwhile student) had missed: 'From henceforth, space by itself, and time by itself, have vanished into the merest shadows and only a kind of blend of the two exists in its own right.'[57]

Minkowski's great discovery was that Einstein's equations of relativity – which look rather obscure in the original 1905 paper – become much easier to understand if they are interpreted in a four-dimensional context. Instead of considering the three dimensions of space separately from the time dimension, Minkowski introduced the notion of a four-dimensional 'spacetime continuum'. This formulation makes it easier to visualise what is going on in Einstein's equations. At high speeds, an object becomes 'rotated' from the spatial dimensions into the time dimension – resulting in the weird effects of length contraction and time dilation already noted by Einstein.

One of the outcomes of Minkowski's work was to demystify that seemingly magical speed c. Why is light always measured to have that particular speed, and why can nothing travel faster than that? According to Minkowski's interpretation everything travels through spacetime (space *and* time – not just space) at exactly the same speed, *c*. A stationary object travels entirely along the *time* dimension. We may think of it colloquially as travelling at 'one second per second' into the future, but in terms of spacetime its speed is *c*. At the other extreme, photons of light – having no mass to hold them back – travel through *space* at that same speed, with no movement along the time dimension. Between the two extremes, moving objects travel partly through space and partly through time – but always with a net speed through spacetime of exactly *c*.

Minkowski published his interpretation of Einstein's theory in 1907, just two years before his untimely death at the age of 44. His contribution was crucial to Einstein's career for two reasons. First having the backing of a respected member of the academic establishment meant that Einstein's work was taken more seriously by the scientific community. Second, Minkowski's concept of a spacetime continuum – formulated in the context of special relativity – was to prove invaluable to Einstein when he moved on to the more difficult problem of *general* relativity.

Einstein's paper 'On the Electrodynamics of Moving Bodies' was published in *Annalen der Physik* at the end of September. Around the same time Einstein sent off a short sequel entitled 'Does the Inertia of a Body Depend upon its Energy Content?', which was duly published in November 1905. At three pages long, the paper is no more than a brief postscript to Einstein's previous article. The gist of it can be summed up in one simple equation, probably the most famous of all time: $E = mc^2$.

In classical physics, energy E and mass m are two completely different concepts. The mass of a body is a measure of the amount of matter it contains, which determines its inertia – the extent to which it resists the action of any force applied to it. Energy, on the other hand, is typically associated with the motion of a body – the faster it moves, the more energy it has.

Einstein showed that energy and mass are essentially equivalent. When an object gains energy as it moves faster, its mass also increases at the same rate. Even when the object is stationary there is hidden energy locked up in its 'rest mass'. Energy and mass are simply different ways of looking at the same thing. Because they are measured in different units, however, you cannot simply write $E = m$. It turns out the conversion factor is the square of the speed of light, c.

The idea that a stationary object should possess an intrinsic energy by virtue of its mass was a startling one. As Einstein himself wrote, at a later date:

E is the energy that is contained in a stationary body; m is its mass. The energy that belongs to the mass m is equal to this mass, multiplied by the square of the enormous speed of light – which is to say, a vast amount of energy for every unit of mass. But if every gram of material contains this tremendous amount of energy, why did it go so long unnoticed? The answer is simple enough: so long as none of the energy is given off externally, it cannot be observed.[58]

As far as Einstein was concerned, that was the end of it. He was not particularly interested in working out how to release the vast amounts of energy locked up in matter. Others could worry about that in due course. In the meantime, however, Einstein's work took him in an altogether different direction.

4

Taking on Newton

'The luckiest thought of my life ...'

Einstein[59]

As he reflected on the events of 1905, Einstein had good reason to feel proud of himself. During the course of the year no fewer than four of his papers had been published in *Annalen der Physik*, and at least two of them – on quantum theory and on special relativity – were unlike anything the world of physics had seen before. Now he just had to sit back and wait for the accolades to pour in. In the words of his sister, Maja, 'Albert imagined that his publication in the renowned and much-read journals would draw immediate attention.'[60]

He was over-optimistic. Prestigious though *Annalen der Physik* was, the fact remained that Einstein was an unknown author without any professional ties to a university or other academic institution; he was still just a patent clerk. And his papers were far from easy reading, based as they were on abstract reasoning rather than laboratory experiment. Maja went on: 'Icy silence followed the publication.'[61]

It was well into 1906 before the ice began to thaw. When it did, it was not as a direct consequence of Einstein's own writings but those of a much better-known scientist, Max Planck (1858–1947). Planck was a pillar of the establishment: Professor of Physics at the University of Berlin, President of the German Physical Society ...

and one of the editors of *Annalen der Physik*. In this last capacity he had read all the papers Einstein had submitted to the journal. Planck had been especially interested in the article about the photoelectric effect, which drew on his own theory of light quanta – but he remained far from convinced by it. Ironically, Planck would be one of the last members of the scientific community to accept Einstein's version of quantum theory.

What struck him right away, however, was Einstein's other big idea: relativity. Planck was one of the few readers who had no problem following Einstein's chain of reasoning, and he could appreciate its logical perfection. He also recognised something Einstein had missed – that relativity was consistent with a basic tenet of theoretical physics called the principle of least action. Dating back to the eighteenth century, this was originally stated by the French philosopher Pierre Maupertuis as 'Nature is thrifty in all her actions'.

Planck's paper on 'The Principle of Relativity and the Fundamental Equations of Mechanics' was published in the *Transactions of the German Physical Society* in April 1906 – and it was this, rather than Einstein's original paper, which first brought relativity to the attention of a wider audience. The following year, Hermann Minkowski published his alternative formulation of Einstein's equations in terms of four-dimensional spacetime, thus adding his weight behind Planck's. With two major establishment figures supporting him, Einstein finally began to receive the recognition he felt he deserved.

Einstein was still just a clerk in a patent office. Early in 1906, soon after he formally received his doctorate, he was promoted from technical expert third class to technical expert second class, but that was as far as it went. He was still tied to his office routine for eight hours a day, six days a week. He continued to churn out scientific papers, though, and his mind continued to grapple with the toughest problems of physics.

The theory of relativity gets its name because it deals with the way the world appears *relative to* an observer in a particular frame of reference. That is not the same as saying that 'everything is relative'. Einstein was actually more interested in things that remained *invariant* for observers who were moving relative to each other – to the extent that he originally wanted to call his discovery 'invariance theory'.[62]

Special relativity was 'special' because it dealt with the specific case of inertial frames of reference, moving at constant velocity. For an observer in an inertial frame, the laws of physics are invariant – that is the essence of special relativity. But something kept nagging at the back of Einstein's mind. Was there a bigger theory out there that still remained hidden – a theory of *general* relativity?

One day in 1907, while he was sitting at his desk in the patent office in Bern, an idea suddenly popped into his head. He later called it '*die glücklichste Gedanke meines Lebens*',[63] which is almost invariably translated into English as 'the happiest thought of my life'. But the German word *glücklich* can mean 'lucky' or 'fortunate' as well as 'happy' –

and indeed this particular thought was to prove extremely fortunate for Einstein's future career.

Einstein's sudden realisation was that there is a particular type of non-inertial frame – one that is accelerating rather than moving at constant velocity – in which the laws of physics are just as invariant as they are in an inertial frame. This is the case of a frame that is falling freely under the action of gravity. The distinctly alarming image that flashed into Einstein's mind was of a scientist trapped in an elevator that was plunging down a lift shaft after the cable had snapped. There was no experiment the scientist could do inside that closed compartment that would distinguish it from a box floating in outer space far from any gravitational field.

Einstein referred to such a frame of reference – falling freely under gravity – as a 'local inertial frame'. From the point of view of someone on the inside, there was no way to distinguish such a frame from a genuine inertial frame. Einstein saw at once that this was the clue he had been looking for, which pointed the way towards a theory of general relativity. It would not be an easy journey, however. Special relativity, from the very first glimmering of an idea to the finished paper, had taken him just five weeks to complete. General relativity would take him eight years.

Although the original impetus for general relativity came out of the special theory, it was not long before it began to pull Einstein in a different direction altogether. If he were to deal with motion in a gravitational field using the same kind of thinking he had employed for special relativity, it meant he would have to develop a new theory of gravity. That was not something Einstein, or anyone else, had been expecting. For more than 200 years the theory of gravity formulated by Isaac Newton had passed every test it had faced. As far as anyone could tell, it was consistent with every astronomical observation that had ever been made and with every experiment carried out on earth.

If Einstein were to make a success of general relativity, it meant he would have to take on Newton. It would be the biggest challenge of his career. As he wrote while he was in the midst of grappling with it:

> I am now working exclusively on the gravitation problem ... But one thing is certain: never before in my life have I troubled myself over anything so much ... Compared with this problem, the original theory of relativity is child's play.[64]

It was not until 1909 that Einstein – now 30 years old and with more than twenty scientific papers to his credit – finally obtained a full-time academic position: an assistant professorship at the University of Zurich. He promptly quit his job at the patent office in Bern, and in October that year he moved back to Zurich with Mileva and their 5-year-old son, Hans Albert.

In July 1910 Mileva gave birth to their second son, Eduard. She liked Zurich and would have been happy to settle down to long-term family life there, but Einstein was ambitious. In Zurich his professorship was a junior one, at almost exactly the same salary he had received from the patent office. He heard that a higher-paying and more prestigious job, as a full professor, was on offer 300 miles away in Prague.

Mileva was unhappy about moving again so soon, but Einstein's career came first. He pursued the Prague job relentlessly, and was overjoyed in January 1911 to hear that he had secured the position – at twice the salary he was getting in Zurich. Two months later he arrived in Prague, reluctantly accompanied by his family.

In Switzerland Einstein had never been much of a family man, and this was even more true in the bustling, cosmopolitan city of Prague. He preferred to spend his evenings mingling with the Bohemian intelligentsia, including the surrealist author Franz Kafka, who, like Einstein, was destined to become one of the defining icons of the twentieth century.

Among the scientific community, Einstein's reputation was beginning to grow. As a consequence of this, he was often invited to travel around Europe to talk about his work. When he did so, he travelled alone – something else that gave Mileva cause for complaint. It was not just that Einstein was away from home so much, but as a former physics student herself she felt she was missing out on something exciting. As she wrote while he was on one of these trips: 'I would have loved only too much to have listened a little and to have seen all these fine people. It has been an eternity since we have seen each other. Will you still recognise me?'[65]

Fortunately for Mileva, Einstein's career as a professor in Prague proved short-lived. Just over a year later he was offered a better job back in Zurich, not at the university this time but at the polytechnic where he and Mileva had first met as students. The position was a good one, with a generous salary. The family moved back to Switzerland in the summer of 1912.

Although Mileva was pleased to be in Zurich once again, it quickly became clear that things were not the same as they had once been. Einstein had changed. As a student he had talked about them working together as intellectual equals, now all he seemed to want her to do was leave him alone and look after the children. Three years earlier, in a letter to a friend, she had said: 'I only hope that fame does not exert a detrimental influence on his human side.'[66] As far as Mileva was concerned, it appeared that her worst fears were coming true.

With Einstein showing so little interest, the marriage was clearly heading towards a crisis. Things came to a head at the end of 1913 when – after just eighteen months in Zurich – Mileva found out they were going to be moving yet again. Einstein had received another tempting offer, this time in Berlin – a professorship again, but one that carried no teaching obligations. Einstein would finally be free to spend as much time as he wanted on research.

The prospect of a move to Berlin had another attraction for Einstein, and another reason for Mileva to despair.

Berlin was where Einstein's 'other woman' lived. Her name was Elsa Löwenthal. She was a divorcee, three years older than him, and they had known each other as children, for the perfectly good reason that they were cousins. Elsa was the daughter of Einstein's mother's sister – which meant, among other things, that she was exactly the sort of 'nice girl' his mother had wanted him to marry in the first place.

Astonishing as it may seem, Elsa and Einstein were related in another way, too. Her father and his father had been first cousins, and her maiden name had been Einstein. Although they had lost touch with each other, Einstein and Elsa got into contact again following her divorce in 1908. She was organised, dutiful and profoundly unimaginative: all the things Mileva was not – and, by this time, all the things Einstein wanted in a wife.

Einstein, Mileva and the two children moved to Berlin in April 1914. They had become a thoroughly dysfunctional family. Mileva was chronically depressed, the children were confused by their parents' constant bickering, and Einstein wanted an end to the marriage. Three months after they arrived in the German capital he produced perhaps the most astonishing document of his life – a unilateral declaration of disdain for his once beloved wife:

> You will make sure that my clothes and laundry are kept in good order; that I will receive my three meals regularly in my room; that my bedroom and study are kept neat, and especially that my desk is left for my use only. You will renounce all personal

relations with me insofar as they are not completely necessary for social reasons. Specifically, you will forego my sitting at home with you and my going out or travelling with you. You will obey the following points in your relations with me: you will not expect any intimacy from me, nor will you reproach me in any way; you will stop talking to me if I request it; you will leave my bedroom or study immediately without protest if I request it. You will undertake not to belittle me in front of our children, either in words or behaviour.[67]

Mileva responded in the only way possible. She quietly packed her bags, got the children together and boarded a train back to Zurich. It was Wednesday, 29 July 1914; just twenty-four hours earlier war had broken out between Austria and her native Serbia. On the following Saturday, Austria's powerful ally Germany declared war on Russia, and then two days later on France. As ever, Switzerland remained resolutely neutral. Mileva was in the safest place she could be – but she no longer had the option of returning to Berlin. The First World War saw to that.

Einstein, meanwhile, was exactly where he wanted to be. He happily set about starting his new life with Elsa and his new career as a senior professor in Berlin. It was not quite plain sailing, though. While his home life was less tempestuous now that Mileva had gone, a new conflict emerged to tax him – a microcosm of the huge conflict that was tearing Europe apart.

Einstein had never liked the idea of war, even when, as a child, he watched other boys playing at being soldiers. As an adult he retained the conviction that all the world's problems could be solved if only everyone would agree to respect each other. Very few of his Berlin colleagues shared this view. German nationalism prevailed, and most of the professors were strong supporters of their government and military. A case in point was Fritz Haber (1868–1934), the head of the chemistry department. He was a good friend of Einstein, who had acted as a kind of diplomatic negotiator with Mileva during her final, fraught days in Berlin. Politically, however, Einstein and Haber were worlds apart. It was Haber, keen to give Germany the technological edge, who first pushed for the use of poisonous gas on the battlefield, thus earning his place in the annals of infamy as the 'father of chemical warfare'.

Shortly after the outbreak of the war, the German government issued a strongly worded proclamation defending its military actions in Europe. It became known as the 'Manifesto of the Ninety-Three', because it was signed by ninety-three prominent academics of the time – including Fritz Haber and Max Planck. Einstein was horrified by the document. Together with another colleague who shared his pacifist convictions, he drafted an alternative *Manifesto to Europeans* proposing the visionary – if entirely unworkable – notion that what humanity really needed was not a world war but a world government:

Progress in technology and communications clearly suggests that we recognise the need for international relations which will necessarily move in the direction of a universal, worldwide civilisation.[68]

Sadly, this was not an idea that many people were prepared to put their name to. The manifesto amassed just four signatures, including those of the two authors.

Einstein's scientific work proved more successful. As soon as he was settled in Berlin he began to make rapid progress with his theory of general relativity, which had been pursued off and on ever since that 'luckiest thought' occurred to him in the Patent Office in 1907. The fully worked-out theory was finally published in the *Proceedings of the Prussian Academy of Sciences* in November 1915.

Virtually every new theory in physics comes about because there is something wrong with the old theory, but that was not the case with general relativity – at least, not at first sight. It is essentially a theory of gravity, and by the early twentieth century Newton's interpretation of that subject was one of the most thoroughly established physical laws in history.

Yet there was a problem with Newtonian gravity, something that had even bothered Newton himself. It was not a problem with the theory's predictive power – it always gave the right answers – but with the model of the world implicit within it. According to Newton, the moon stays in its orbit around the earth because it feels a gravitational force acting on it – yet the earth and the moon are separated by some 250,000 miles of empty space. It looked like a case of 'action at a distance', and it had baffled Newton and everyone who followed him.

Einstein's theory solved the problem in a way no one had expected: it eliminated the very notion of a gravitational force. In the absence of a force, an object travels in a straight line at constant speed – that is the essence of Newton's first law of motion. And, contrary to all indications, that is exactly what Einstein said was happening when the moon orbits the earth.

The key lies in the concept of four-dimensional spacetime – which had been invented by Einstein's old teacher Hermann Minkowski in the context of special relativity, but which Einstein embraced wholeheartedly in his development of general relativity.

If Minkowski's spacetime can be likened to a flat sheet of rigid material, then the spacetime of general relativity is like a flexible rubber sheet which distorts in the vicinity of massive objects. The shortest distance between two points – technically called a geodesic – is always a straight line in flat space, but in a distorted space it may not be. An object moving through such a space may follow a curved trajectory even if there are no forces acting on it. As the American physicist John Wheeler succinctly put it: 'Matter tells spacetime how to curve, and curved space tells matter how to move.'[69]

General relativity is a mathematical tour de force. It is extremely complicated, but it succeeds in explaining all the phenomena of gravity in terms of 'straight line' – or, rather, geodesic – trajectories in curved spacetime. Even today, however, very few physics students are taught general relativity as undergraduates for the simple reason that its consequences, in virtually all situations of practical interest, are identical to those of Newton's much simpler theory. Whether you view the moon as attracted to the earth by a mysterious 'force of gravity' or as travelling along a geodesic in curved spacetime, the answer is exactly the same.

No one could deny that Einstein's new theory was very clever, and it certainly caught the attention of his peers in the physics community, but that was as far as it should have gone. There was no reason for ordinary people to take an interest in Einstein's work, which had far less relevance to everyday life than developments in the field of electronics being made at the same time.

Whatever else Einstein might have expected when he published his paper on general relativity, one consequence was to exceed his wildest dreams. Within a few years the work had propelled him to international celebrity – a status he would retain for the rest of his life.

5

An Unlikely Celebrity

'One of the highest achievements of
human thought ...'

J.J. Thompson on Einstein's prediction of the
bending of light by the sun[70]

Einstein's separation from Mileva, which had lasted the duration of the First World War, finally became permanent with a divorce settlement in February 1919. This left him free to marry the woman he had been living with since 1914. On 2 June 1919 Elsa Löwenthal (*née* Einstein), Albert's maternal and paternal cousin, became his second wife as well.

Following his remarriage, Einstein's relationship with his ex-wife and their two children – which had become distinctly fraught during the time they were still married but living apart – gradually improved. In 1915 he had written of Hans Albert: 'My fine boy has been alienated from me for the past few years by my wife, who has a vengeful disposition.'[71] By 1924 he could write to Mileva: 'We should put all the bad things behind us. You should enjoy what life has given you – like wonderful children, the house and that you are not married to me any more.'[72]

The elder of the two sons, Hans Albert, studied engineering at the Zurich polytechnic where his parents had met. Initially Einstein had hoped Hans Albert would follow in his own footsteps, but then changed his mind: 'Science is a difficult profession. Sometimes I am glad that you have chosen a practical field, where one does not have to look for a four-leaf clover.'[73]

The younger son, Eduard, studied psychology at Zurich University. He became a keen follower of Sigmund Freud, leading him to some introspective musings on the father-son relationship: 'It's at times difficult to have such an important father, because one feels so unimportant.'[74] For his part, Einstein Senior remained unconvinced by Freudian psychology. When Freud and Einstein met in Vienna in 1927, they found they agreed wholeheartedly about politics but little else. 'Einstein understands as much about psychology as I do about physics,' was the way Freud put it.[75]

Sadly, Eduard was to develop psychological problems of his own. He became subject to fits of depression and was diagnosed with schizophrenia. From his mid-twenties onwards he had to be increasingly cared for by his mother, even spending time in a mental institution when his illness became particularly severe.

Around the time of Einstein's divorce and remarriage, high drama was being played out elsewhere in the world – and it revolved around the unlikely subject of general relativity. Almost all the consequences of Einstein's theory were very similar to Newton's law of gravity – so similar, in fact, that the difference was too small to be measured. There was an important exception, however, which related to the bending of a light beam as it passed close to a massive object. Newton's theory predicted one value for the amount of bending, while general relativity predicted twice that value.

Einstein realised that if a star was observed close to the sun during a solar eclipse when the sun itself was hidden by the moon, the star's measured position would be shifted relative to where it would appear if the sun were not there. The predicted size of the shift was different in the two theories, and the difference should be large enough to be measurable. Back in 1915 Einstein had set down a challenge to astronomers to measure the size of the shift, and see whether it agreed with Newton or with himself.

The challenge was eventually taken up, in 1919, by a British astronomer named Arthur Eddington (1882–1944). He was drawn to it for two reasons: one scientific, the other political. As a scientist, he was one of the earliest supporters of relativity, and had written the first English-language book on the subject, published in 1918. But Eddington had something else in common with Einstein: he was a lifelong pacifist. He felt that if a British scientist was the first to confirm the theory of a German scientist – in the immediate aftermath of a long and destructive war between the two countries – it would convey a message of peace and reconciliation.

A total eclipse was due to take place in May 1919, but it would only be visible from certain, rather inaccessible parts of the globe. Eddington was undaunted. He sent one team of observers to the remote city of Sobral in Brazil, while he led a second team to the small island of Principe off the west coast of Africa.

With the aid of powerful telescopes, both teams managed to take a number of photographs during the course of the eclipse. Unluckily for Eddington's team, the weather at Principe was cloudy, and all but two of the photographs from that site turned out to be unusable. The weather at Sobral was clear, but the extreme heat caused problems with the telescope optics, and the resulting images were fuzzy.

With substandard photographs from both sites, measuring the shift in star positions was harder than expected. While some of the measurements did appear to agree with Einstein, others were closer to the predictions of Newton's theory.[76] Nevertheless, Eddington decided – largely on the basis of his personal expectations – that the weight of evidence fell in Einstein's favour.

The formal announcement of the results took place at the Royal Society in London on 6 November 1919. The packed meeting was chaired by the society's president, J.J. Thomson, the man who had discovered the electron in 1897. The eclipse measurements were presented not by Eddington, but by the Astronomer Royal, Sir Frank Dyson, who concluded by giving them his seal of approval:

> The results of the expeditions to Sobral and Principe leave little doubt that a deflection of light takes place in the neighbourhood of the sun and that it is of the amount demanded by Einstein's generalised theory of relativity.[77]

Adding his own endorsement, J.J. Thompson remarked, 'This is one of the most important results obtained in connection with the theory of gravitation since Newton's day. It is one of the highest achievements of human thought.'[78]

The following morning *The Times* carried an account of the meeting under the dramatic headline:

REVOLUTION IN SCIENCE
New Theory of the Universe
NEWTONIAN IDEAS OVERTHROWN[79]

The story was soon picked up by other newspapers, and rapidly made its way around the world. Media and public alike were gripped by relativity fever. It was a much-needed 'good news' story after so many years of unremitting gloom. People were captivated by the idea of those two great adversaries, Britain and Germany, collaborating on such a peaceful, positive endeavour – just as Eddington had hoped they would be.

The focus, as the last line of *The Times* headline suggests, was on the supposed overthrow of Newton's theory of gravity. At the time Newton symbolised the pinnacle of scientific genius in much the same way Einstein does today. The thought that his ideas might have been 'proved wrong' was too enticing for any editor to pass over.

Later that month, *The Times* approached Einstein for his own views on the subject. The result was a long essay entitled 'What is the Theory of Relativity?', which duly appeared in the newspaper on 28 November 1919. In it Einstein focuses on the development of relativity as an exercise in deductive logic, rather than attempting to explain discrepancies in existing theories:

> The new theory of gravitation diverges considerably, as regards principles, from Newton's theory. But its practical results agree so nearly with those of Newton's theory that it is difficult to find criteria for distinguishing them which are accessible to experience ... The chief attraction of the theory lies in its logical completeness ... Let no-one suppose, however, that the mighty work of Newton can really be superseded by this or any other theory.[80]

The world, however, felt differently. Newton's rigidly clockwork universe was a thing of the past. Relativity meant a new kind of freedom; space itself was warped, and who knew what the implications might be? In the immediate aftermath of the First World War such ideas had a particular resonance with the spirit of the time. Einstein's theory was lumped together with the burgeoning avant-garde movement: the cubist paintings of Picasso, the dissonant music of Stravinsky and the surreal novels of Kafka, Einstein's friend from his days in Prague. In such a climate the fact that relativity was seen as a difficult or obscure theory was no obstacle at all – in fact it was a positive boon.

Einstein's physical appearance added to the illusion that he belonged to the artistic rather than the scientific set. A professor in those days was expected to be neatly turned out in a suit and tie – unlike this rather scruffy individual with wayward hair and baggy clothes.

Before long Einstein was being hounded by press reporters and photographers wherever he went. He often moaned about this, but there is little doubt that he really liked the attention he was getting. As the author C.P. Snow wrote:

> There was a streak in him that enjoyed the photographers and the crowds. He had an element of the exhibitionist and the ham. If there had not been that element, there would have been no photographers and no crowds. Nothing is easier to avoid than publicity.[81]

Einstein was soon travelling the world. The initial motivation for this, however, had nothing to do with science or relativity but rather with politics. He was approached by an activist named Chaim Weizmann (1874–1952) to support his campaign for a Jewish homeland in the Middle East. Weizmann was a Russian-born biochemist who had emigrated to Britain at the age of 30. During the First World War he became Director of the Admiralty Laboratories, a position which gave him the ear of the British establishment. Weizmann campaigned relentlessly for a Jewish homeland, and by the end of the war this had begun to look like a viable prospect. With the fall of the Ottoman Empire, the British Government took control of Palestine and – in Article 95 of the Treaty of Sèvres – expressed the ultimate aim of establishing a 'national home for the Jewish people'.

Weizmann's movement to create the modern state of Israel became known as Zionism, and it left Einstein with mixed feelings. On the one hand he disliked any kind of nationalism – throughout his life he was what might be termed an 'internationalist'. On the other hand, he was alarmed by the sudden rise of anti-Semitism in Europe, and felt an increasingly close kinship with his fellow Jews. It became clear to him that there would be serious problems as long as they remained a diaspora within Europe. In the end, because he liked and admired Weizmann, he decided to support him.

Characteristically, Einstein's understanding of Middle East politics tended towards the naïve. A colleague from Einstein's later years, Ernst Straus, put it in the following way:

He felt that when there was trouble in a colonial country it was due to the colonial power promoting strife. He was firmly convinced that in India there would have been no trouble between Muslims and Hindus if it had not been for the British government. Similarly, in Palestine he believed that the quarrel between Jews and Arabs was largely due to the British.[82]

Einstein's first trip with Weizmann was to the United States, with the primary aim of raising money for the

Zionist cause. They arrived in April 1921, and Einstein was greeted in New York with the enthusiasm normally accorded to a movie star. Crowds lined the streets to watch him drive past, and everyone wanted to hear his opinions. He was the perfect crowd-puller for Weizmann. As Einstein himself put it: 'I am needed not for my abilities but solely for my name, from whose publicity value a substantial effect is expected.'[83]

Britain was Einstein's next stop. After arriving in Liverpool on 8 June, he travelled the short distance to Manchester University where he delivered two lectures: the first on relativity and the second on Zionism. The university awarded him an honorary doctorate. Einstein then proceeded to London where he was greeted by some of the country's leading scientists, including Eddington and J.J. Thomson, as well as such public figures as the playwright George Bernard Shaw and the Archbishop of Canterbury. The latter earnestly enquired as to the moral implications of relativity, to which Einstein replied bluntly: 'It makes no difference. It is purely abstract science.'[84]

Einstein's globetrotting had only just begun. The following year, 1922, he visited France and the Far East. In 1923 he travelled to Palestine, Spain and Scandinavia. In 1925 he toured South America. The whole world opened its arms to the man who had given it the theory of relativity.

Or perhaps not quite the whole world. A small but vocal minority of scientists remained vehemently opposed to relativity, for a very sinister reason. Einstein was a Jew, and there was a rising tide of anti-Semitism in the German-speaking world. One of the most outspoken members of the anti-Einstein faction was the physicist Philipp Lenard – the man whose work on the photoelectric effect had led, back in 1905, to Einstein's first major scientific paper.

In the early days Lenard had written favourably about Einstein's work. Later, however, he became outraged by Einstein's pacifist utterances and by the public adulation he received in the wake of his theory of relativity. Lenard also came to hold the irrational belief that Germany's Jews had been responsible for the country's defeat in the First World War. He convinced himself that relativity was a 'Jewish theory' and hence, by definition, wrong.

It was almost certainly due to the influence of Lenard, who had won the Nobel Prize in 1905, that Einstein repeatedly failed to receive that accolade – despite being the world's most honoured scientist in so many other respects. By the time the news came, in November 1922, that he had finally won the Nobel Prize, Einstein – now more celebrity than scientist – was in the middle of a tour of Japan.

The citation on Einstein's Nobel Prize refers not to the theory of relativity but to his earlier work on quantum physics and the photoelectric effect. This may seem like a deliberate snub, but the actual reason is probably more subtle. In those days the Nobel Prize was almost never awarded for purely theoretical work, which is essentially what relativity was. Indeed, the chairman of the Nobel Committee referred to Einstein's work on relativity as being closer to philosophy than physics. Quantum theory, by contrast, is much more deeply rooted in experimentation and has important practical applications in the field of electronics. Modern solar cells, for example, work on the principle of the photoelectric effect.

Einstein's work in quantum physics led to another practical application – one everyone has heard of. In 1916, a year after general relativity, he published a paper entitled 'Emission and Absorption of Radiation in Quantum Theory'. It introduced a completely new concept, which he called stimulated emission, whereby a photon of light hitting an atom can produce a second photon with identical properties to the first. The laser, short for 'Light Amplification by Stimulated Emission of Radiation', is the best-known consequence of this theory.

Although Einstein was one of the great pioneers of quantum theory, by the middle of the 1920s the subject was moving in a direction with which he was uncomfortable. The new development was called quantum mechanics and it had swept up most of the world's physicists in a tidal wave of enthusiasm. Einstein was virtually alone in his opposition.

To a physicist, the word 'mechanics' refers to the way physical objects move and interact with each other. The classical mechanics of Newton – and of Einstein himself, for that matter – are rigidly prescriptive; at any given time an object has both a clearly defined position and a clearly defined momentum. According to quantum mechanics, this is not the case on a subatomic scale. Instead of being clearly defined, there is a fundamental fuzziness in the definitions of position and momentum, as expressed in Werner Heisenberg's notorious 'uncertainty principle' of 1927.

Einstein disliked the idea of uncertainty. Revolutionary as he was, he wanted his universe to be clearly defined. He had the perfect chance to air his views in October 1927 when a major gathering of the world's physicists took place in Brussels. This was the fifth in a series of such conferences named after the Belgian philanthropist Ernst Solvay; as a young man Einstein had attended the first Solvay conference in 1911.

The 1927 Solvay conference was a dramatic affair. At 48, Einstein was one of the oldest people there, and almost the only one who remained unconvinced by quantum mechanics. Attendees witnessed his countless clashes with the leading proponents of the new theory: Heisenberg himself and the Danish physicist Niels Bohr (1885–1962). Einstein put forward a series of thought experiments to get his point of view across, but each time his arguments were successfully refuted by his opponents. As Heisenberg later put it:

Einstein would bring along to breakfast a proposal of this kind … By dinner time we could usually prove that his thought experiments did not contradict uncertainty relations. But next morning he would bring along to breakfast a new thought experiment, generally more complicated than the previous one.[85]

To Einstein's credit, he seems to have accepted defeat graciously whenever Bohr and Heisenberg showed him the flaw in his argument. He was prepared to concede battles, but that was not the same as giving up the war. He doggedly refused to accept the idea of a probabilistic universe, expressing his oft-quoted view that 'God does not play dice'. But Bohr had an answer to that one, too: 'Einstein, stop telling God what to do!'[86]

Twenty years earlier Einstein had been a young rebel fighting against the scientific establishment. Now the tables were turned. He could at least appreciate the irony of the situation: 'To punish me for my contempt of authority, Fate has made me an authority myself.'[87]

6

The Grand Old Man of Science

'Displayed on various occasions as an oddity ...'

Einstein on himself[88]

In the early days of general relativity the subject was often described as being so difficult that only a handful of scientists in the world were capable of understanding it. That sounded like a challenge, and over the coming years many people set themselves the task of getting to grips with Einstein's theory. One of them was a Belgian priest, Monseigneur Georges Lemaître (1894–1966). He spent his later years in the Vatican as president of the Pontifical Academy of Sciences, but in the 1920s he was a junior member of staff at the Catholic University of Leuven.

Using the equations of general relativity, Monseigneur Lemaître came up with an audacious new model of the universe. First described in 1927, Lemaître's universe started out as just a microscopic point, which he called the 'cosmic egg', before expanding to its present dimensions. That was just the start of it. According to Lemaître, the universe was still expanding.

When Einstein saw the Belgian priest's work, it struck him as ridiculous. But he was forced to admit he could find no fault in Lemaître's reasoning: 'Your ideas are correct, but your physics is abominable,' he declared.[89] Einstein's own solution, which had been produced as far back as 1917, was a perfectly static universe. From a mathematical point of view it was somewhat more contrived than Lemaître's expanding universe. In order to make it work, Einstein had to introduce an arbitrary factor into the equations which he called the 'cosmological constant'.

Lemaître was right and Einstein was wrong. Lemaître's 'cosmic egg' is now known as the Big Bang, and it is still the most widely accepted model of the universe. Einstein's static model had started to look untenable as early as 1929, when the American astronomer Edwin Hubble found that the universe is indeed expanding, just as Lemaître's model said it should be.

One of the earliest champions of the Big Bang model, George Gamow, quoted Einstein as saying that the introduction of the cosmological constant 'was the biggest blunder he ever made in his life'.[90] In hindsight, the blunder was not so much Einstein's cosmological constant – which does make an appearance in current theories – but his dogmatic assertion that Lemaître's model could not possibly be correct, even though he knew there was nothing wrong with its mathematics.

If a Catholic priest seems an unlikely protagonist in the story of relativity, then the British philosopher Bertrand Russell (1872–1970) is equally implausible. Best known for his work on logic and the philosophy of language, Russell was one of the first non-physicists to grapple with the technicalities of general relativity. In 1925 he produced a popular account of the subject called *The ABC of Relativity*, which drew copious praise from Einstein himself.

Russell had an ulterior motive for promulgating relativity. He wanted to make the world a more peaceful place, and he believed that applying the principles of relativity to social and political issues would reduce the likelihood of conflict. Like Einstein, Russell was a committed pacifist – he had argued passionately against Britain's involvement in the First World War and ended up spending six months in prison for his beliefs.

Einstein and Russell became lifelong friends, united both by their political beliefs and their shared interest in science and philosophy. For Einstein, pacifism had come to mean more than simply opposition to war – it meant a commitment on the part of individuals to refuse to fight for their country under any circumstances. He expressed this view in dramatic terms in 1930, on his second visit to the United States:

> The timid might say, 'What's the use? We shall be sent to prison.' To them I would reply: Even if only two per cent of those assigned to perform military service should announce their refusal to fight ... governments would be powerless, they would not dare send such a large number of people to jail.[91]

Within days, pacifist sympathisers across America were proudly sporting badges inscribed with a new slogan: 'Two per cent'.

While Einstein was travelling around the world with his message of peace, at home in Germany the anti-Semitic views of people like Philipp Lenard had not abated – in fact they had grown much more intense. A Scottish scientist, Lancelot Law White, noticed this when he visited Einstein in Berlin:

> It was quite impossible for Einstein then – and I am speaking of 1928 to 1929 – to fail to be conscious of the fact that he was already perhaps the dominant symbol for anti-Semitism in Germany, so that it was really uncomfortable for him to remain there.[92]

The situation came to a head in January 1933, when the openly anti-Semitic Nazi party came to power. Jewish books – including Einstein's – were publicly burned in a Berlin square and Adolf Hitler appointed Einstein's bête noire Philipp Lenard as his new chief scientist. Shortly afterwards, Einstein was declared an enemy of the state. His picture was posted with the words 'Not Yet Hanged' printed under it.[93]

Fortunately Einstein missed all this excitement, having been away on yet another of his American tours since the previous December. He did return to the continent one last time, but got no closer to Germany than the little town of De Haan on the Belgian coast, where he rented a house for a few months during the summer of 1933. There were growing concerns that Hitler might invade Belgium (which he eventually did, in 1940) and Einstein became so worried by this possibility that he decided, in the specific case of the Nazis, to compromise his hitherto uncompromising pacifism:

Were I a Belgian, I would not, in the present circumstances, refuse military service; rather, I would enter such service cheerfully in the belief that I should thereby be helping to save European civilisation.[94]

As for Einstein personally, it had become clear that his future lay elsewhere than Europe. The previous year he had been offered a post in Princeton, New Jersey. He now decided the time had come to accept the offer. Princeton was home to one of the oldest and most distinguished universities in the United States, but Einstein's new job was at a neighbouring, brand-new establishment called the Institute for Advanced Study. There, as in Berlin, Einstein would be free to pursue his research without the bother of teaching commitments.

Einstein arrived in New Jersey in October 1933. He was accompanied by his secretary, Helen Dukas, who had worked for him since 1928, and by his second wife, Elsa. Shortly after their arrival Elsa began to develop a serious illness. The relationship between the two had always been a very practical one – Einstein needed someone to look after him – so Elsa was pleasantly surprised by her husband's reaction to her misfortune: 'He went around miserable and depressed. I never thought he was so attached to me.'[95]

Elsa died in 1936, after which responsibility for looking after the great man fell largely on Helen Dukas. From 1939 onwards she was aided by Einstein's younger sister, Maja, who came over from Europe to live with him in Princeton. In 1938, Einstein's son Hans Albert also emigrated to America. He worked for several years in South Carolina before moving to California to take up a post as Professor of Hydraulic Engineering.

***

By the 1930s a stark dichotomy had become apparent in theoretical physics. On one side there was general relativity, which provided an explanation for gravity; on the other there was quantum mechanics, with its explanation of electromagnetism and nuclear forces. Unfortunately, the two theories were incompatible with each other. There was a widespread feeling that there ought to be a single 'theory of everything' – either an extension of quantum mechanics to encompass gravity, or an extension of relativity to encompass electromagnetism and nuclear forces.

Einstein was almost alone in believing that the route to a theory of everything lay via the second approach; he was as convinced as ever that quantum mechanics was wrong and that he had been on the right track with relativity. He referred to his vision as the unified field theory, and he pursued it relentlessly during the last twenty years of his life. He never succeeded – and even in the twenty-first century scientists are still seeking that elusive grail.

Unlike Einstein, most physicists today expect the long-sought theory, if and when it finally emerges, to be a development not of general relativity but of quantum mechanics – a subject Einstein himself never fully accepted. One of the things he objected to was Heisenberg's uncertainty principle: the idea that it is impossible to measure both the exact position and exact momentum of a particle at the same time. Einstein felt instinctively that there must be a way to do this – and in 1935, during a conversation with a young Princeton colleague named Nathan Rosen, he thought he finally saw how it could be done.

As so often with Einstein, his sudden insight took the form of a thought experiment. Suppose two particles, A and B, interact with each other in such a way that their quantum states become intimately related to each other. In modern parlance this is called 'quantum entanglement', although the term did not exist in the 1930s. If A and B subsequently become separated by a large distance, there is no longer any obvious way they can interact with each other. This is the so-called 'principle of locality', which Einstein took to be self-evident.

According to the uncertainty principle, we can choose to measure either the momentum of a particle or its position, but not both. So let us measure the momentum of A and the position of B. Then, because we know the two particles are entangled, we can calculate the momentum of B based on the measured momentum of A. So now we know both the position of B *and* its momentum – in flat contradiction of Heisenberg's uncertainty principle.

The only way to rescue Heisenberg is to do away with the principle of locality – by supposing that B somehow *knows* that A has had its momentum measured, the very instant the measurement takes place. This idea struck Einstein as preposterous: 'Physics should represent a reality in time and space, free from spooky action at a distance.'[96]

Another Princeton physicist, Boris Podolsky, offered to write up the thought experiment on behalf of Einstein and Rosen. It became known as the 'EPR paradox' after the paper's three authors: Einstein, Podolsky and Rosen. The paper's title took the form of a question: 'Can Quantum-Mechanical Description of Physical Reality be Considered Complete?' The authors themselves clearly believed the answer was negative. Even before it appeared, Podolsky had leaked the article to *The New York Times*, which summarised it under a screaming headline:

EINSTEIN ATTACKS QUANTUM THEORY
Scientist and Two Colleagues
Find It Is Not 'Complete'
Even Though 'Correct'[97]

It was not until the 1980s – long after Einstein's death – that it became technically possible to carry out experiments to resolve the situation one way or the other. The answer, when it came, was clear. Quantum mechanics is correct; locality is an illusion.

At first sight this looks like a defeat for Einstein, but in a deeper sense it can be seen as one of his greatest triumphs. Using the same relentless logic that led him to the theory of relativity, he had devised the ultimate test of quantum mechanics to reveal a profound and counter-intuitive truth about the universe. The only thing Einstein got wrong, on this occasion, was to put his money on the losing side.

As it turned out, Einstein was not very happy with the EPR paper: 'It did not come out as well as I had originally wanted,'[98] he complained. The problem was not the argument itself – which he firmly believed – but the obscure way in which Podolsky had presented it. On top of that, Einstein was furious that Podolsky had sent the paper to *The New York Times* without consulting his two co-authors. It is said that Einstein never spoke to Podolsky again.

Einstein did, however, continue his collaboration with Nathan Rosen for several more years. Perhaps their most important discovery together came as an offshoot of the quest for a unified field theory – a way to incorporate electromagnetism into the framework of general relativity. While they were attempting to grapple with this problem, they discovered it was possible, under certain circumstances, for a kind of 'shortcut' to exist between two points that are widely separated in spacetime. Initially such a short cut was referred to as an Einstein-Rosen bridge, but this has now been superseded by the more evocative term 'wormhole'. While they may or may not exist in the real universe, wormholes have become a staple of science fiction – they provide a convenient way for authors to get round the speed-of-light limitation imposed by Einstein's theory of special relativity.

While Einstein was engrossed in theory, other physicists were addressing more practical issues. A group of them

– working quite openly, with no particular concern for secrecy – had discovered a way to release at least some of the enormous energy implied by Einstein's equation $E = mc2$. It involved creating a chain reaction among nuclei in a particular form of the element uranium. The result would be an 'atom bomb' of unprecedented destructive power.

One of the scientists involved in this work was the Hungarian Leo Szilárd (1898–1964), who had been a colleague of Einstein's in Berlin. He moved to the United States in 1938, and around that time a worrying thought occurred to him: what would happen if the Nazis decided to make an atom bomb? The Germans understood the theory as well as anyone else, since it had been published openly. All they needed was uranium – and Szilárd thought he could see how they might obtain it. There were vast uranium deposits in the Congo which, being under Belgian administration at the time, might easily fall into Nazi hands.

Szilárd had to find a way to stop the Germans acquiring uranium. He knew that Einstein was on friendly terms with the Queen of Belgium, so he decided to visit Einstein, who was on vacation on Long Island. The idea of a chain reaction took Einstein by surprise: he had seen none of the work on the subject, and the possibility had never crossed his mind. But he grasped it immediately and saw the immense danger to the world if an atom bomb fell into Hitler's hands.

After further discussion they decided that warning the Belgians was not the best way forward; as guests in

America it would be unwise for them to deal with a foreign government. It was agreed that Einstein would sign a letter, drafted by Szilárd, that would be sent to no less a person than the President of the United States – Franklin D. Roosevelt. Furthermore, the letter would not merely warn of the German threat, but it would urge America to take proactive action on uranium research.

Einstein's letter to Roosevelt was delivered in August 1939. It had the desired effect: in October that year the Advisory Committee on Uranium held its first meeting. The committee would eventually evolve into the Manhattan Project – an all-out effort to develop an atom bomb ahead of the Nazis. The rest, of course, is history: America built a bomb, Germany did not.

Because of his prominent political role, Einstein is sometimes referred to as the 'father of the atom bomb'. But that simply is not true, as he was quick to point out:

I do not consider myself the father of the release of atomic energy. My part in it was quite indirect. I did not, in fact, foresee that it would be released in my time. I believed only that it was theoretically possible. It became practical through the accidental discovery of chain reaction, and this was not something I could have predicted.[99]

Nor did Einstein have any involvement in the Manhattan Project. With his outspoken pacifism and internationalism, there was no way the US Government would have cleared him for top secret work. The spokeswoman for one conservative group claimed that 'Not even Stalin himself is affiliated with so many anarcho-communist international groups'.[100]

This was the official position, too. Einstein had been viewed as a security risk from the moment he entered the country. By 1940 the FBI had classified him as an 'extreme radical'[101] and generated a detailed file on him stretching to 1,500 pages. Since his arrival in the United States, Einstein had extended his politics to encompass civil liberties and social justice as well as pacifism. When the famous African-American singer Marian Anderson was refused a hotel room in Princeton simply on the basis of her skin colour, Einstein put her up in his own house. The two became good friends, and the singer visited Einstein on many subsequent occasions.

After the war Einstein became extremely worried by the prospect of future conflicts fought with atomic weapons. His proposed solution was characteristic: 'The secret of the bomb should be committed to a world government, and the United States should immediately announce its readiness to give it to a world government.'[102] Expanding on this theme to a newspaper reporter, he said:

> The only salvation for civilisation lies in the creation of world government, with security of nations founded upon law … As long as sovereign states continue to have separate armaments and armaments secrets, new world wars will be inevitable.[103]

By the time Einstein entered his seventies, in 1949, he was starting to feel increasingly out of step and isolated: 'I have become a lonely old fellow. A kind of patriarch ... displayed on various occasions as an oddity.'[104] Many of his friends and former colleagues were dead. He was out of touch with modern trends in physics and bewildered by current events. His health was poor; he had been diagnosed with a potentially fatal heart weakness. The previous year his first wife, Mileva, had died in Switzerland, and their schizophrenic younger son Eduard – who until then had been cared for by his mother – had been put into a mental asylum.

The biggest blow came in June 1951, when Albert's sister Maja died. She had been living with him in Princeton for the previous twelve years – the last real tie to his family roots. Einstein was heartbroken: 'I miss her more than can be imagined,'[105] he wrote.

Another death, which affected Einstein in a completely different way, occurred in November 1952. The victim in this case was Chaim Weizmann, the man who had drawn Einstein into the campaign for an independent Jewish state after the First World War. The campaign had eventually proved successful, and the new country of Israel had come into existence in 1948. Weizmann had become its first president, although the role was essentially that of a figurehead; the day-to-day running of the country fell to its prime minister, David Ben-Gurion.

With Weizmann dead the country needed a new figurehead. For Ben-Gurion there was one obvious choice:

'If we are looking for a symbol, why not have the most illustrious Jew in the world, and possibly the greatest man alive – Einstein?'[106]

By this time Einstein's health was far too frail for him to consider moving to Israel in order to take up such a high-profile position. He made that clear to anyone who would listen. But diplomacy has its rules. To Einstein's amusement, Israel insisted on going ahead with a formal offer of the presidency. Einstein received it on 17 November and responded, in equally formal terms, the following day. His stated reason for declining was not poor health but unsuitability for the position:

> All my life I have dealt with objective matters, hence I lack both the natural aptitude and the experience to deal properly with people and to exercise official function.[107]

At least one of Einstein's elderly friends was still enjoying the best of health. The philosopher Bertrand Russell, now in his eighties, was as lively as ever. Always a pacifist, he was now firmly aligned with the campaign for nuclear disarmament. Early in 1955 he approached Einstein with the idea of getting a number of prominent scientists to sign a declaration he had drafted on the subject. Einstein welcomed the idea, and suggested the names of scientists he thought should be invited to sign the document.

Einstein himself signed the declaration – now known as the Russell–Einstein manifesto – on 11 April 1955.

The following day his secretary, Helen Dukas, found him collapsed and in agony. His heart, which had been weak for years, was finally failing. Einstein was rushed to hospital, but there was little hope for him. Less than a week later he was dead.

The joint manifesto with Bertrand Russell became Einstein's final testament, and it shows that he remained idealistic to the end:

In view of the fact that in any future world war nuclear weapons will certainly be employed, and that such weapons threaten the continued existence of mankind, we urge the governments of the world to realise, and to acknowledge publicly, that their purpose cannot be furthered by a world war, and we urge them, consequently, to find peaceful means for the settlement of all matters of dispute between them.[108]

7

Einstein's Legacy

'He was the pre-eminent scientist in a century dominated by science.'

Time magazine on Einstein[109]

With the death of Albert Einstein, a life in the service of science and humanity which was as rich and fruitful as any in the whole history of our culture has come to an end. Mankind will always be indebted to Einstein for the removal of the obstacles to our outlook which were involved in the primitive notions of absolute space and time.[110]

So wrote Niels Bohr, Einstein's long-time adversary in his intellectual duels over quantum mechanics, in the June 1955 issue of *Scientific American*. Two months earlier, on 19 April – the day after Einstein's death – *The New York Times* had carried a lengthy obituary. It included the following observation:

Paradoxically, as the years passed, the figure of Einstein the man became more and more remote, while that of Einstein the legend came ever nearer to the masses of mankind. They grew to know him not as a universe-maker whose theories they could not hope to understand but as a world citizen, one of the outstanding spiritual leaders of his generation, a symbol of the human spirit and its highest aspirations.[111]

By the time the obituary appeared, Einstein's body had already been cremated and his ashes scattered in an undisclosed location. His funeral, attended by just a few close friends and family members, had been held on the afternoon of the day he died. Only one press photographer was present, from *Life* magazine, and only one of the pictures he took that day – of Einstein's cluttered office, just the way he left it – was published at the time. The other photographs, at the request of Einstein's family, remained unpublished and were soon forgotten. They were rediscovered, and belatedly published, more than half a century later.[112]

In the brief hours between Einstein's death and his cremation, the body was autopsied by a Princeton hospital pathologist named Thomas Harvey. Secretly, without even informing Einstein's family, Harvey held on to Einstein's brain. He later claimed this was in response to Einstein's own request that his brain should be retained for scientific study. Whether this is true or not is unknown. In any case, what ensued was something of a farce. Harvey chopped the brain up into small sections, some of which he passed to other researchers but most of which he kept for himself, in jars intended for food storage. The question everyone wanted to answer, of course, was whether the physical residue of Einstein's brain held any clues to the origin of his extraordinary genius. With the brain no longer intact, however, serious study was impossible. The various examinations that were carried out on it came to conflicting conclusions. Some said that Einstein's brain did indeed display some peculiar features, others that it was perfectly ordinary.

After his death, Einstein's transition from man to myth – already hinted at in *The New York Times* obituary – continued unabated. As science historians Alan Friedman and Carol Donley put it in 1985: 'Albert Einstein has come to represent intelligence in general, and the scientific mind in particular.' They go on to say that popular images of Einstein invariably portray him as a very old man: 'The Einstein who discovers relativity in the popular image is at least forty years older than the Einstein who invented relativity in fact. The association of wisdom with age is a longstanding notion … so if Einstein is to represent intellectual wisdom for our culture, he had better be much older than a tender twenty-six years.'[113]

Today's users of social media are often confronted with Einstein 'memes' – usually taking the form of a picture of the very old Einstein, along with a photoshopped caption putting one pithy utterance or another into his mouth. Perhaps the most pertinent of these reads: 'I never said half the crap people say I did.' He probably never said that, either.

Einstein did not, for example, say 'Two things inspire me to awe: the starry heavens above and the moral universe within'. It is a striking and thought-provoking sentiment, and it was indeed said by one of history's greatest thinkers: the eighteenth-century German philosopher Immanuel Kant. But few people today have heard of Kant, so to attribute the quotation correctly would involve a long explanation of who Kant was and why his ideas carry weight. It is so much simpler to attribute the words to Einstein instead!

Sometimes the misattributions take a more sinister form. The Kant quotation is consistent with Einstein's actual utterances, so it is something he *might* have said. The following, however, is a different matter:

> Astrology is a science in itself and contains an illuminating body of knowledge. It taught me many things, and I am greatly indebted to it. Geophysical evidence reveals the power of the stars and the planets in relation to the terrestrial. In turn, astrology reinforces this power to some extent. This is why astrology is like a life-giving elixir to mankind.

This statement, although frequently attributed to Einstein in books about astrology, is completely at odds with his actual belief.[114] The quotation above, complete with its spurious attribution, has been traced to a German astrological calendar published in 1960 – 'an excellent example of a quotation someone made up and attributed to Einstein in order to lend an idea credibility'.[115] The quotation has since acquired a life of its own, repeated ad nauseam by people too lazy to check its authenticity.

Alongside the wrongly attributed quotations, there are dozens of Einstein myths and misconceptions in circulation, such as the notion that Einstein was hopeless at mathematics when he was at school – when in fact it was one of his best subjects. In 1935, a friend showed him a syndicated newspaper feature in the *Ripley's Believe It or Not!* series: 'Greatest Living Mathematician Failed in Mathematics.' As Einstein himself was quick to point out: 'I never failed in mathematics. Before I was fifteen I had mastered differential and integral calculus.'[116]

With regard to Einstein's work, the theory of relativity has a particular tendency to attract misinterpretation. A surprising number of people feel qualified to object to Einstein's theory without the need to understand it. Since the earliest days when Philipp Lenard and the Nazi party denigrated relativity as 'Jewish science', the objections have often been politically rather than scientifically motivated. In the minds of many people there is no real distinction between Einstein's relativity and the socio-political concept of 'cultural relativism'. This association is spurious, although it was promoted on occasion by Einstein's own supporters, including Bertrand Russell.

Probably because Einstein is one of the few scientists people have heard of, he is one of the commonest targets for pseudoscientists trying to prove 'the scientific establishment' wrong. As science writer Brian Clegg puts it:

People like proving Einstein wrong. There's something of an industry devoted to this, and I've lost count of the number of books I have been sent with some novel physics theory that shows that the great man was mistaken.[117]

The deductive method used by Einstein can reach a false conclusion in one of two ways: either because the starting premise is wrong or because the subsequent logic is flawed. Einstein's errors were of the first kind. If he reached an incorrect conclusion, it was usually because he started out with a false assumption; his logical reasoning was normally impeccable.

Einstein famously described his introduction of the cosmological constant into the equations of general relativity as his 'biggest blunder'. He took it for granted that the universe was static – neither contracting or expanding – and the cosmological constant was necessary to ensure this would be the case. Einstein's only 'blunder' lay in this assumption of a static universe; his subsequent logic was correct, and further discoveries in recent decades have shown that his equations do indeed require such a factor.

Einstein's opposition to quantum mechanics – which now lies at the very heart of modern physics – might also be seen as one of his 'mistakes'. But this misses an important point: his arguments against the theory actually helped rather than hindered its development. As his biographers Michael White and John Gribbin put it:

Simply by providing such carefully reasoned opposition ... and forcing Bohr, Bohm and others to come up with new ideas in response to his arguments, Einstein ensured that the theory was put on a more secure footing, more quickly, than would otherwise have been the case. That was certainly not his intention; but in the role of quantum opponent he made yet another invaluable contribution to science.[118]

The repercussions of Einstein's scientific legacy continue to this day. One of the predictions of general relativity – one which has no counterpart in Newton's theory of gravity – is the existence of gravitational waves: ripples in the fabric of spacetime which propagate like waves on the ocean. Detecting such waves, if indeed they exist, is one of the greatest challenges of modern physics. Although there is tantalising indirect evidence, to date they have never been detected directly. To borrow a term from electrical engineering, the 'signal-to-noise ratio' is simply too small. Nevertheless, dogged attempts are being made to improve the sensitivity of gravitational wave detectors, and many scientists believe the elusive discovery will be made in the not-too-distant future.

It is possible, in fact, that the 'discovery' has already been made, but that the evidence is languishing unseen in the masses of data already collected. To this end a collaborative project called *Einstein@Home* was set up in 2005, in which volunteers around the world allow their home computers to sift through data from gravitational wave detectors. As the project's website says:

Einstein@Home uses your computer's idle time to search for weak astrophysical signals from spinning neutron stars (also called pulsars) using data

> from the LIGO gravitational-wave detectors, the Arecibo radio telescope, and the Fermi gamma-ray satellite … Our long-term goal is to make the first direct detections of gravitational-wave emission from spinning neutron stars. Gravitational waves were predicted by Albert Einstein almost a century ago, but have never been directly detected. Such observations would open up a new window on the universe, and usher in a new era in astronomy.[119]

Ironically, that 'biggest blunder' of Einstein's also plays a crucial role in modern physics. Added to the equations of general relativity, the cosmological constant – usually represented by the Greek letter lambda – can be thought of as a kind of uniform 'pressure' pervading the whole universe. Einstein gave lambda a negative value (negative pressure) in order to prevent the universe from expanding, because he took it for granted that it had to be in a steady state. Soon afterwards, however, astronomers discovered that the universe was indeed expanding. The immediate assumption was that the value of lambda was precisely zero, and that the whole idea of a cosmological constant had been an unnecessary complication. This was what Einstein was referring to when he talked about his 'biggest blunder'.

That was not the end of the story, though. If the universe was expanding, the gravitational pull of all the matter inside it should cause the rate of expansion to slow down over time. In 1998, however, it was discovered that the opposite was true: the universe was expanding at an ever-accelerating pace. The easiest way to explain this observation was by reinstating the cosmological constant, but this time with a positive value (positive pressure) instead of negative. The currently favoured cosmological model is referred to by the name Lambda-CDM. Lambda refers to the fact that there is indeed a non-zero cosmological constant, while CDM stands for Cold Dark Matter – another component of the model. Lambda is sometimes referred to by the equally sinister-sounding term 'dark energy'.

In non-scientific matters, too, Einstein left a lasting legacy. The Russell–Einstein Manifesto, which he signed just a week before his death, was formally released three months later by its co-author Bertrand Russell, at a press conference in London on 9 July 1955. Signed by nine prominent intellectuals in addition to Einstein and Russell, the declaration was a fervent plea against the use of the 'H-bomb' – the hydrogen bomb that would be '2,500 times as powerful as that which destroyed Hiroshima'. The manifesto went on to paint a stark picture of the realities of nuclear war, with its threat of worldwide radioactive fallout:

No one knows how widely such lethal radioactive particles might be diffused, but the best authorities are unanimous in saying that a war with H-bombs might possibly put an end to the human race. It is feared that if many H-bombs are used there will be universal death, sudden only for a minority, but for the majority a slow torture of disease and disintegration.[120]

Unlike many well-intentioned declarations of this type, the Russell-Einstein manifesto had a practical, lasting impact. Two years later, in July 1957, Russell and one of the other signatories – a Polish physicist named Joseph Rotblat – inaugurated a series of conferences aimed at reducing or eliminating the threat posed by nuclear weapons. These became known as the Pugwash Conferences, after the location of the first conference – a small coastal town in Nova Scotia – and they continue to this day. In 1995, forty years after the Russell-Einstein manifesto, Joseph Rotblat and the Pugwash Conferences received the Nobel Peace Prize 'for their efforts to diminish the part played by nuclear arms in international politics and, in the longer run, to eliminate such arms'.[121]

In May 2015, a poll of almost 7,000 students around the world found that Albert Einstein was considered history's greatest hero – ahead of religious figures like Jesus Christ and the Buddha, fellow scientists like Isaac Newton, and political campaigners like Mahatma Gandhi, Martin Luther King and Nelson Mandela.[122]

Another poll that Einstein won was carried out in November 1999, among a hundred of the world's leading physicists. The question on this occasion was 'who was the greatest physicist of all time?' Galileo finished in sixth place, Heisenberg in fifth, Bohr fourth, Maxwell third,

Newton second – each of them an undisputed genius who made huge steps forward in our understanding of the physical world. But none of them stood in quite the same league as Einstein. As one of the participants, theoretical physicist Brian Greene, explained: 'Einstein's special and general theories of relativity completely overturned previous conceptions of a universal, immutable space and time, and replaced them with a startling new framework in which space and time are fluid and malleable.'[123]

Einstein was a great scientist, and the full ramifications of his discoveries are still being worked out today. He provides an inspiration to people around the world, both as a symbol of scientific creativity and for his idealistic passion. But these things alone are not quite enough to explain Einstein's status as one of the most instantly recognisable human beings who ever lived. Ultimately, Einstein is more than a mere person: he is the personification of his age. As the editors of *Time* magazine said in December 1999, when they named him Person of the Century:

He was the pre-eminent scientist in a century dominated by science. The touchstones of the era – the Bomb, the Big Bang, quantum physics and electronics – all bear his imprint.[124]

Notes

1   Einstein, Albert, *Ideas and Opinions* (Souvenir Press, 2005), p.226.
2   Balibar, Françoise: *Einstein: Decoding the Universe* (Thames & Hudson, 2001), p.13.
3   Isaacson, Walter, *Einstein: His Life and Universe* (Pocket Books, 2008), p.118.
4   Einstein, *Ideas and Opinions*, p.226.
5   Balibar, *Einstein: Decoding the Universe*, p.45.
6   Whitrow, G.J. (ed.) *Einstein, the Man and his Achievement* (Dover, 1973), p.30.
7   Isaacson, *Einstein: His Life and Universe*, p.222.
8   White, Michael & Gribbin, John, *Einstein, a Life in Science* (Simon & Schuster, 1994), p.140.
9   Balibar, *Einstein: Decoding the Universe*, p.104.
10 *Ibid.*, p.134.
11 Isaacson, *Einstein: His Life and Universe*, p.280.
12 Bernstein, Jeremy, *Einstein* (Fontana, 1973), p.22.
13 Isaacson, *Einstein: His Life and Universe*, p.427.
14 Bernstein, *Einstein*, pp.177–8.
15 Isaacson, *Einstein: His Life and Universe*, p.335.
16 See for example Isaacson, *Einstein: His Life and Universe*, chapter 17.
17 *Ibid.*, p.297.
18 www.bbc.co.uk/sn/tvradio/programmes/horizon/einstein_symphony_prog_summary.shtml.
19 White & Gribbin, *Einstein, a Life in Science*, p.216.
20 www.nobelprize.org/nobel_prizes/physics/laureates/1921/press.html.

21   Cox, Brian & Forshaw, Jeff, *Why Does E=mc2?* (Da Capo Press, 2009), pp.235–7.

22   Bernstein, *Einstein*, p.13.

23   White & Gribbin, *Einstein, a Life in Science*, p.209.

24   Isaacson, *Einstein: His Life and Universe*, p.439.

25   White & Gribbin, *Einstein, a Life in Science*, p.191.

26   Isaacson, *Einstein: His Life and Universe*, p.426.

27   *Ibid.*, p.186.

28   *Ibid.*, p.518.

29   *Ibid.*, p.150.

30   Wishinsky, Frieda, *Albert Einstein* (DK Publishing, 2005), p.104.

31   White & Gribbin, *Einstein, a Life in Science*, pp.7–8.

32   *Ibid.*, p.39.

33   Wishinsky, *Albert Einstein*, p.10.

34   *Ibid.*, p.14.

35   Isaacson, *Einstein: His Life and Universe*, p.11.

36   White & Gribbin, *Einstein, a Life in Science*, p.34.

37   Isaacson, *Einstein: His Life and Universe*, p.34.

38   White & Gribbin, *Einstein, a Life in Science*, p.39.

39   Isaacson, *Einstein: His Life and Universe*, p.33.

40   *Ibid.*, p.42.

41   *Ibid.*, p.45.

42   *Ibid.*, p.51.

43   *Ibid.*, p.74.

44   *Ibid.*, p.118.

45   *Ibid.*, p.75.

46   *Ibid.*, p.86.

47   White & Gribbin, *Einstein, a Life in Science*, p.48.

48   Isaacson, *Einstein: His Life and Universe*, p.98.

49   *Ibid.*, p.118.

50   *Ibid.*, p. 74.

51 *Ibid.*, p.137.

52 Whitrow, *Einstein, the Man and his Achievement*, p.19.

53 Isaacson, *Einstein: His Life and Universe*, p.136.

54 Cox & Forshaw, *Why Does E=mc2?*, pp.1–2.

55 *Galileo: Selected Writings* (Oxford World's Classics, 2012), pp.271–2.

56 Isaacson, *Einstein: His Life and Universe*, p.128.

57 Cox & Forshaw, *Why Does E=mc2?*, pp 1–2.

58 Einstein, *Ideas and Opinions*, pp.339–40.

59 White & Gribbin, *Einstein, a Life in Science*, p.127.

60 Wishinsky, *Albert Einstein*, p.59.

61 Isaacson, *Einstein: His Life and Universe*, p.140.

62 *Ibid.*, p.132.

63 White & Gribbin, *Einstein, a Life in Science*, p.127.

64 Balibar, *Einstein: Decoding the Universe*, p.53.

65 Wishinsky, *Albert Einstein*, p.69.

66 Isaacson, *Einstein: His Life and Universe*, p.154.

67 *Ibid.*, p.186.

68 White & Gribbin, *Einstein, a Life in Science*, p.119.

69 Isaacson, *Einstein: His Life and Universe*, p.220.

70 Wishinsky, *Albert Einstein*, p.78.

71 Isaacson, *Einstein: His Life and Universe*, p.210.

72 *Ibid.*, p.276.

73 *Ibid.*, p.277.

74 *Ibid.*, p.366.

75 *Ibid.*, p.366.

76 See for example Clegg, Brian, *Gravity: Why What Goes Up, Must Come Down* (Duckworth Overlook, 2012), pp 135–6.

77 Isaacson, *Einstein: His Life and Universe*, p.261.

78 Wishinsky, *Albert Einstein*, p.78.

79 Isaacson, *Einstein: His Life and Universe*, p.264.

80 Einstein, *Ideas and Opinions*, pp.231–2.

81 Isaacson, *Einstein: His Life and Universe*, pp.268–9.

82 Whitrow, *Einstein, the Man and his Achievement*, p.87.

83 Balibar, *Einstein: Decoding the Universe*, p.76.

84 White & Gribbin, *Einstein, a Life in Science*, p.160.

85 Isaacson, *Einstein: His Life and Universe*, p.346.

86 *Ibid.*, p.326.

87 *Ibid.*, p.317.

88 Wishinsky, *Albert Einstein*, p.108.

89 www.lefigaro.fr/sciences/2014/04/03/01008-20140403 ARTFIG00219-albert-einstein-avait-il-tout-prevu.php.

90 Isaacson, *Einstein: His Life and Universe*, p.356.

91 *Ibid.*, p.371.

92 Whitrow, *Einstein, the Man and his Achievement*, p.56.

93 Wishinsky, *Albert Einstein*, p.98.

94 White & Gribbin, *Einstein, a Life in Science*, p.207.

95 Wishinsky, *Albert Einstein*, p.103.

96 Isaacson, *Einstein: His Life and Universe*, p.450.

97 www.ias.edu/about/publications/ias-letter/articles/2013-fall/epr-fallout.

98 Isaacson, *Einstein: His Life and Universe*, p.450.

99 Einstein, *Ideas and Opinions*, p.121.

100 Isaacson, *Einstein: His Life and Universe*, p.399.

101 White & Gribbin, *Einstein, a Life in Science*, p.240.

102 Einstein, *Ideas and Opinions*, p.118.

103 Balibar, *Einstein: Decoding the Universe*, p.87.

104 Wishinsky, *Albert Einstein*, p.108.

105 Isaacson, *Einstein: His Life and Universe*, p.518.

106 White & Gribbin, *Einstein, a Life in Science*, p.244.

107 Isaacson, *Einstein: His Life and Universe*, p.522.

108 pugwash.org/1955/07/09/statement-manifesto/.

109 content.time.com/time/magazine/article/0,9171,993017,00.html.

110 www.scientificamerican.com/article/einstein-obituary-arti/.

111 www.nytimes.com/learning/general/onthisday/
bday/0314.html.

112 time.com/3494553/the-day-albert-einstein-died-a-
photographers-story/.

113 Balibar, *Einstein: Decoding the Universe*, p.132.

114 Isaacson, *Einstein: His Life and Universe*, p.384.

115 Denis Hamel: 'The End of the Einstein-Astrology-
Supporter Hoax', *Skeptical Inquirer*, November 2007.

116 Isaacson, *Einstein: His Life and Universe*, p.16.

117 Clegg, *Gravity: Why What Goes Up, Must Come Down*,
p.108.

118 White & Gribbin, *Einstein, a Life in Science*, pp.225–6.

119 Einstein@Home: einstein.phys.uwm.edu/.

120 pugwash.org/1955/07/09/statement-manifesto/.

121 pugwash.org/1995/12/10/oslo-award-of-the-nobel-
peace-prize/.

122 www.dailymail.co.uk/sciencetech/article-3090109/
Bush-hated-Stalin-Einstein-bigger-inspiration-Jesus-
Study-reveals-history-s-heroes-villains.html.

123 Einstein the Greatest: http://news.bbc.co.uk/1/hi/sci/
tech/541840.stm.

124 content.time.com/time/magazine/
article/0,9171,993017,00.html.

Timeline

1879	Born on 14 March in Ulm, Germany
1885	Starts school in Munich, where the family now live
1894	Left alone in Munich when his family moves to Italy
1895	Renounces German citizenship and moves to Switzerland
1900	Graduates from Zurich Polytechnic
1902	Begins work at the Swiss Patent office in Bern
1903	Marries Mileva Marić
1905	Has several important scientific papers published, including one on special relativity
1906	Receives his doctorate from Zurich University
1907	Has his 'luckiest thought' that will lead to general relativity
1909	Becomes an associate professor at Zurich University
1911	Moves to Prague where he is made a full professor
1912	Returns to Zurich, this time as a full professor at the polytechnic
1914	Obtains a good position in Berlin, but Mileva returns to Zurich soon afterwards

1915	Finalises the theory of general relativity
1916	Publishes a paper laying the groundwork for the development of lasers
1919	Divorces Mileva and marries his cousin Elsa; Eddington's eclipse expedition provides observational support for general relativity
1921	First visits to the United States and Britain
1922	Awarded the 1921 Nobel Prize for physics
1927	Clashes with the proponents of quantum mechanics at the Solvay conference
1933	Emigrates to the United States, where he takes up a position at the Institute for Advanced Study in Princeton
1935	Formulates the 'EPR paradox' in collaboration with Podolsky and Rosen
1939	Signs a letter addressed to President Roosevelt alerting him to the possibility of an atom bomb
1952	Declines the presidency of Israel when it is offered to him
1955	Dies on 18 April, a week after signing the Russell–Einstein manifesto

Further Reading

Balibar, Françoise, *Einstein: Decoding the Universe* (Thames & Hudson, 2001)

Bernstein, Jeremy, *Einstein* (Fontana, 1973)

Clegg, Brian, *Gravity: Why What Goes Up, Must Come Down* (Duckworth Overlook, 2012)

Cox, Brian & Forshaw, Jeff, *Why Does E=mc2?* (Da Capo Press, 2009)

Einstein, Albert, *Ideas and Opinions* (Souvenir Press, 2005)

Einstein, Albert & Infeld, Leopold, *Evolution of Physics* (Cambridge University Press, 1971)

Isaacson, Walter, *Einstein: His Life and Universe* (Pocket Books, 2008)

White, Michael & Gribbin, John, *Einstein, a Life in Science* (Simon & Schuster, 1994)

Whitrow, G.J. (ed.), *Einstein, the Man and his Achievement* (Dover, 1973)

Wishinsky, Frieda, *Albert Einstein* (DK Publishing, 2005)

Web Links

einsteinpapers.press.princeton.edu/ – An extensive online collection of Einstein's papers.

www.aip.org/history/einstein/ – Information about Einstein from the American Institute of Physics.

content.time.com/time/magazine/ article/0,9171,993017,00.html – A collection of articles from *Time* magazine about the 'Person of the Century'.

www.ias.edu/people/einstein – Einstein's life at the Institute for Advanced Study in Princeton.

physics.aps.org/story/v15/st11 – Short article about wormholes and the 'Einstein-Rosen bridge'.

Giuseppe Verdi Henry V **Brunel** Pope John Paul II **Jane Austen** Sigmund Freud **Abraham Lincoln** Robert the Bruce **Charles Darwin** Buddha **Elizabeth I** Horatio Nelson **Wellington** Hannibal & Scipio **Jesus** Joan of Arc **Anne Frank** Alfred the Great **King Arthur** Henry Ford **Nelson Mandela** Edward Jenner **Napoleon Bonaparte** Isaac Newton **Albert Einstein** John Lennon **Elizabeth II**